Reiki

for everyday living

Reiki
for everyday living

Eleanor McKenzie

Bounty
Books

Publisher: Samantha Warrington
Editorial & Design Manager: Emma Hill
Editor: Anna Southgate
Designer: Leah Germann
Production Controller: Sarah Kramer

This edition reprinted in 2016

First published in 2014 by Bounty Books,
a division of Octopus Publishing Group Ltd
Carmelite House
50 Victoria Embankment
London EC4Y 0DZ
www.octopusbooks.co.uk

An Hachette UK Company
www.hachette.co.uk

Material previously published in *The Reiki Bible* (Gaia, 2009)

Reprinted in 2015

ISBN: 978-0-753728-32-1

A CIP catalogue record for this book is available from the
British Library

All reasonable care has been taken in the preparation of this book, but the
information it contains is not meant to take the place of medical care under the
direct supervision of a doctor. Before making any changes in your health regime,
always consult a doctor. Any application of the ideas and information contained
in this book is at the reader's sole discretion and risk.

CONTENTS

INTRODUCTION

With origins in various Eastern traditions, including Buddhism, Reiki is a form of hands-on healing, in which energy is drawn from the Universe and transmitted through the palms of the hands to achieve a rebalancing of life force. Reiki is very easy to learn and can be used to heal every aspect of our lives. We can administer Reiki to ourselves and to others. It is a practice that cures ills, soothes emotions and enables us to create the life that we want.

REASONS TO PRACTISE REIKI

There are many reasons to practise Reiki, the most common one being the desire to heal others, while others will choose it because it is a holistic system for healing oneself. Both are valid reasons.

BENEFITS OF REIKI

Regardless of the motivation each person has for wanting Reiki in his or her life – and each individual's reasons are right for them and not to be judged or compared with others – there are many benefits that come with the practice. First of all, these will be felt on a physical and emotional level. Reiki supports the body's ability to heal itself by restoring its energy balance. It strengthens the immune system so that all types of illnesses can be resisted, or at least overcome more quickly. It can also be used as a treatment for a number of conditions (see Chapter 4) and it is one of the most effective reducers of stress that can be used by the individual without having to seek treatment elsewhere. It can also be used with other therapies (Chapter 5).

Once we feel better physically, we are often more able to turn our attention to the less tangible issues we face. On an emotional level, it promotes a sense of being at peace with oneself, and can also, sometimes painfully, reveal the root cause of our feelings and behaviour. Yet Reiki, no matter how challenging the cleansing process, always teaches us that nothing ever stays the same. What seems like despair today can be transformed into relief tomorrow as we release the emotional baggage that has been weighing us down.

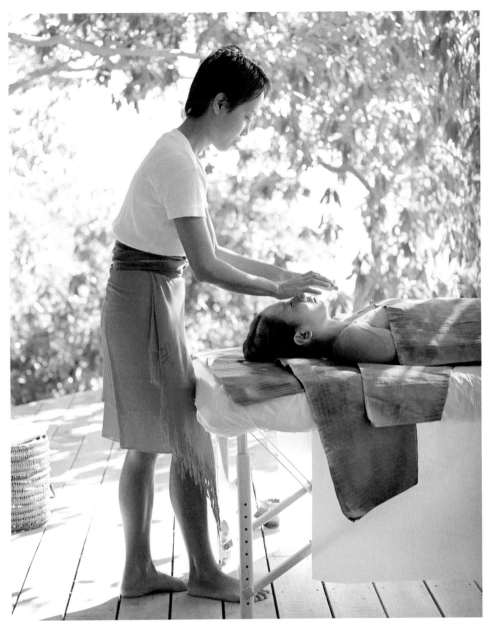

Reiki has origins in 19th-century Japan. It is still practised there today, although forms differ from Western variations.

USING THIS BOOK

There are three stages – called degrees – to developing Reiki. The first allows you to heal yourself and others; the second enables you to achieve that healing from a distance; and the third allows you to teach the practise of healing to others.

The focus of this book is the first degree, but it also offers an ideal foundation from which to continue on to the second and third degrees, should you wish.

The main sections of this book are arranged as follows:

- An introduction to the basic principles of Reiki.

- An overview of energy and how it relates to our body systems.

- The Reiki hand positions for treating yourself and others

- Instruction for healing common conditions

- Using other therapies alongside Reiki.

The system of Reiki is so flexible, with numerous ways to incorporate it into your lifestyle, that you will always be able to find an approach that suits you. There are no rules telling you that you 'must' do this or that.

Instead, you are in charge. There is nothing forced upon you in Reiki. You take responsibility for your practice and develop it at your own pace.

Added to this, Reiki can be applied to an astonishing number of facets of your life. You can give Reiki to all your family members, as demonstrated in this book. But you can also give Reiki, to your pets and your home. Everyone and everything around you can be included in your practice.

While not essential, it is advisable to take a course from an instructor before getting started. That way you will become familiar with the hand positions more speedily, and will have undergone at least one attunement (see page 26).

YOU ARE THE CENTRE

It is important to remember to keep yourself at the centre of your practice. Strengthening yourself will change the way in which you experience the world. Family relationships will improve or resolve themselves for the good of everyone. Problems will melt away as your perspective on them changes. Once you are practising regularly, you will have a tool to work with, so that when you are faced with a challenge, no matter how mundane, you will have the confidence to trust that the outcome is perfect for your life.

Reiki is a flexible system that puts you at the centre, and that you can develop at your own pace.

TAKING THE
FIRST STEPS

Taking the first steps on your journey with Reiki opens up a new world of healing experiences that range from healing yourself and others to healing your home and healing the world.

ENERGY

The Universe is energy. Out of energy everything is created. The energy your body is created from is the same as that of a mountain. It may seem incomprehensible that an object that appears to be lifeless and unchanging could have the same origins as a plant that is living, growing and constantly developing, yet that which is fragile is from the same source as that which is dense. This energy unites the Universe.

UNIVERSAL LIFE FORCE

The concept of a universal life force can be found in a number of Eastern traditions. In Indian Ayurvedic medicine and in yoga it is called *Prana*; in traditional Chinese medicine, which is based on Taoism, it is called *Chi* or *Qi*, which then became *Ki* in Japanese. According to Mantak Chia in his book, *Awaken Healing Light of the Tao*, this life force can be defined as energy, air, breath, wind and vital essence. In short, it is the activating energy of the Universe. When this energy is removed from a body or a plant, life has departed.

Although other cultures have long accepted the idea of a universal energy, or life force, that permeates everything, Western culture has been more reluctant to accept such an idea. First, beliefs about the nature of the Universe were strongly influenced by a religion in which humans were superior to the rest of Creation, and the concept of a God who created the world but who 'lived' outside it. Second, as science developed, and the idea of God became more questionable in many minds, people demanded proof before an idea could be accepted.

Over the last 50 years, physicists have been investigating matter, and have come to the conclusion that underlying all matter, in all forms, is energy. This energy vibrates at different rates, and it is because of this that a rock is more solid and dense than a human body. The idea that everything is formed from one energy source is very important when it comes to working with energy through Reiki. If everything in the Universe is created from one source, then all things, animate or inanimate, are connected. This means that we are constantly interacting with and influencing each other.

One of the wonders of the world is that everything is created from the same universal life force: trees, mountains, oceans, machines and human beings.

WORKING WITH ENERGY

Although the energy of the Universe is unlimited, within living creatures it is not. In the Chinese practice of Chi Kung it is believed that we are born with an abundance of energy. When we are young, we are able to replenish our energy reserves; as we get older, we use up energy but are unable to replace it with the same ease. The result of this is a lack of energy, which can cause ill health. Working with energy to reverse, or at least mitigate, this loss is found in a number of practices.

For example, Chi Kung teaches that through practising a series of movements we can cultivate energy and bring ourselves back into a state of balance. In yoga, the breathing practice called *Pranayama* produces the same result.

With the practice of Reiki, energy is drawn from the Universe and transmitted through the palms of the hands to achieve a rebalancing of life force. Being in this state of balance enables us to find contentment and to sense our connectedness to everything around us.

Being in a state of balance, as symbolized by Yin/Yang, enables us to enjoy life fully.

Feel the build-up of energy.

It must be pointed out that working with energy is not about having a belief in God, or any religion. Working with energy can simply come from the desire to improve your life in all ways. It can be combined with a spiritual practice, or it can be a form of spiritual practice itself.

It is then to spiritual traditions such as Taoism, Buddhism and Hinduism that we must look for the physical and mental practices that will teach us about energy work, and its power to heal our own lives, and the lives of others. It seems ironic that Jesus is considered by many, and not just Christians, to have been the greatest healer, and yet for almost 2,000 years nobody listened to what he said about healing, believing instead that it was a divine gift available only to him. Yet Jesus clearly said, when he baptized the apostles with the Holy Spirit (which seems remarkably similar to the form of energy attunement used in the teaching of Reiki, see page 26), that everyone could heal themselves, and others, in the way that he did.

Basic energy exercise

If you are a complete novice to energy work, or simply wish to experience the reality of energy, here is a very basic way to experience energy as something we can feel and work with.

1 Raise your hands in front of you at just below eye level, with your palms facing each other and about 30 cm (1 ft) apart.

2 Slowly push the palms towards each other until they are about 15 cm (6 in) apart, then bring the palms back to their original position.

3 Repeat this action several times, until you can feel the build-up of energy between the palms. When you try to bring your palms together, you should feel some resistance from the energy between your hands.

WHAT IS HEALING?

The English word 'heal' comes from the Anglo Saxon word *hal*, which primarily meant 'whole', but it also meant 'healthy' and 'holy'. In modern times, these words have lost their connection to each other, just as Western culture has, for the most part, lost the connection between health and wholeness.

In Western medicine, it is generally accepted that there is no 'soul dimension' to disease. Disease originates in the physical body, or the environment, and treatment focuses on the body. The mind has come to play a bigger part in doctors' thinking about the outcomes of treatments; but, while they may accept that a positive attitude can influence the results of treatment, this is seen as a random effect rather than an integral element of the healing process.

With body, mind and spirit disconnected, there can be no complete healing. A soul that is sick will manifest its 'disease' ultimately as physical symptoms. Alternative therapies diverge from conventional medicine in their understanding of the origins of disease. The therapist sees the patient as being more than a body. Therefore, they also seek to treat the spirit within, which is the key source of imbalance in our minds and bodies.

BECOMING CONNECTED

Being healed is to become connected once more to the soul. This may not always result in a complete physical healing. It may be that the healing is such that it allows the person to approach the transition of the soul from the body in a way that helps them to understand their life, complete their journey and accept their imminent death. We should not, therefore, confuse being healed with necessarily being in good health.

At the heart of all healing there is love and compassion. The act of wishing to heal yourself or another is an act of love and compassion. When we are disconnected from love, we become disconnected from others; when we are connected to love, we feel closer to people and to nature. Through love we become One. Through Reiki we can connect with love, and express it with compassion both to ourselves and others.

Plato believed that complete healing must have a 'soul' dimension and that the body, mind and spirit all needed treatment holistically.

Reiki can help us to understand the root causes of any disease that afflicts us. The thoughts and feelings we have about ourselves and the world are the chief cause of our suffering. Yet we must learn to explore these beliefs with compassion and without guilt, and without judging the people who gave us these beliefs, such as 'I am not good enough'.

'The cure of the part should not be attempted without treatment of the whole. No attempt should be made to cure the body without the soul... this is the error of our day, that physicians first separate the soul from the body.'

Greek philosopher Plato, 427-347 BCE

HANDS ON OR PALM HEALING

We all use our hands to heal. When we touch someone to reassure them, or give them a hug, or kiss to make the pain go away, we are applying the comfort of touch, but we are also transmitting an energy to the other person that will help them to heal. Anyone who does energy work will be aware of this. However, those who are not involved in this work have perhaps only an inkling that there is something more powerful than just showing concern behind their instinct to touch a person or animal in distress.

Many people are aware that if they put their hands on their stomach when it hurts after a while it feels somewhat better. Their hands may get warmer, but they don't know why. This is not because they have a special talent – we can all transmit this energy to ourselves and others by placing our hands on the body.

The laying-on of hands, as it is sometimes called, for the purpose of healing, is a tradition in almost every society and culture. Some believe that healers are given a special gift from God. It is true that some spiritual and intuitive healers are able to draw sufficient energy for healing direct from the source without training in a practice such as Reiki. However, most people are using their own energy when they put their hands on themselves or another person to heal them. In the long run, this depletes their own store of *Ki*,

Often when we comfort someone by hugging them or touching them in some way, we are unknowingly using our hands to heal them.

Hands-on healing is a dominant aspect of Reiki practice.

and can lead to illness. This is why it is important to learn a practice such as Reiki.

TAP INTO FAST-FLOWING ENERGY

The hands-on healing of Reiki, or 'palm healing' as it translates from the Japanese word *tenohira*, is by no means the only system of transmitting healing energy, but it is unique in the simplicity of learning the method. Compared with other practices, the Reiki energy is immediately accessed by the practitioner. Added to this, the energy flows fast and strong for most people from the moment of their first attunement (see page 26), and can be accessed instantly the practitioner has the intention to use it. This makes it an ideal practice for the majority of people.

THE HAND POSITIONS

Hand positions occasionally vary between schools of Reiki but the rules are simply a guide. The essence of the practice is in allowing the wisdom of the energy to guide your hands. (See Chapter 3 for a step-by-step guide to the hand positions).

HEALING EXPERIENCES AND RESPONSES

A person's experience of a Reiki treatment and the way they respond is unique to them. So, if you are new to giving treatments to other people, don't expect to see a uniform response, and don't expect your experience of channelling the energy to be the same every time either.

One early experience of my own with the variations in energy came when my teacher asked for volunteers to help her give Reiki at an exhibition. I was working with an experienced practitioner, when a man approached the stand and asked for a treatment. When I put my hands on his shoulders to connect with the energy, I remember thinking it had a different shape to any I had experienced before. When I visualized the energy I could see jagged peaks, whereas when I had visualized the energy in other people it always seemed to be like rounded waves. I talked to the other practitioner about it afterwards. She asked me if this was the first man I had given Reiki to, and I replied it was. Her opinion was that I was seeing very strong male energy that was in stark contrast to the female energy I was used to.

Not everyone will experience the difference between male and female energy in the same way. This was my experience, and an early one in my practice, but it was certainly useful in teaching me that I could expect to find differences between people, and between treatments.

KEEPING AN OPEN MIND

Some people seem to absorb and flow with the energy during a treatment, whereas others may resist. Some people have dramatic visual experiences, while others may experience strong physical sensations. Some simply see changing colours, and others have no recollection of what they experienced. Whatever the experience, you can be sure that the person is receiving healing – perhaps not in the way they expect, and possibly not in the way you expect, because even though we should have no expectations about the process we very often do.

Expectations limit healing. When we are young we learn by using our

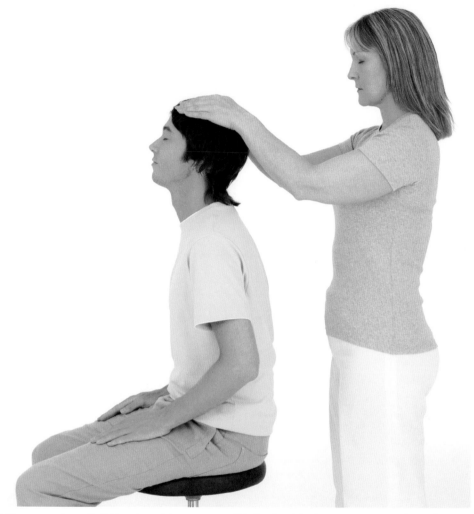

When you give a Reiki treatment to someone, it is best not to have any expectations about how they will respond.

logical mind: if you touch something hot it will burn you, so once experienced we avoid repeating it. When it comes to healing we cannot apply the same logic. Suppose you are treating a specific condition and you observe a particular response. The temptation of logic is to look for a similar response the next time you treat the same condition. However, healing is unique to the individual and requires us to keep our minds open.

USING THE FIRST DEGREE

This book is concerned with using the first level of Reiki – known as the First Degree. It can be used in so many ways. The only thing that is missing from this level is the ability to send distance healing, which is learned in the Second Degree. Therefore, many people find that the First Degree is sufficient in itself.

First Degree Reiki can be used for:

- self-healing
- healing others
- healing animals and plants
- bringing energy to your environment
- energizing food and drink.

SELF-TREATMENT

Self-healing is the most important first step in Reiki, because without healing yourself you cannot heal others. Giving yourself Reiki every day is an essential part of this. I always ask students to give themselves a full self-treatment every day for the first 21 days after their First Degree class. Of course, I would like it if they continued with daily self-treatments after this period, but

I realize that not everyone has time for a full treatment every day. The 21-day period after any class is the most important for clearing old energy and bringing yourself into balance.

The hand positions for self-treatment are shown in Chapter 3. Each position should be held for approximately 3–5 minutes, but if you need to hold a position for longer follow your intuition. If you don't have time for a full treatment every day, a little Reiki is better than none. The more you give yourself Reiki, the more familiar and at ease you will become with the energy and the length of time you need to hold each position.

When to practice

Make yourself comfortable when giving yourself a treatment. Your bed or the sofa are the best options. Some people like to give themselves a treatment before getting out of bed; others prefer last thing before going to sleep. It all depends on what suits you. Although if you do choose last thing at night it is unlikely you will get through a full treatment before falling asleep.

Banishing doubt

The effects of self-treatment are cumulative. The more regular your practice, the more benefits you will feel. There may be times when you don't want to bother giving yourself Reiki. This is normal, but if this attitude persists please take a moment to consider what is behind it. Perhaps you are feeling that you don't deserve time for yourself, or maybe you are letting life dictate a pace that you would rather not have, but which you can see no way out of. Whatever the reason is, don't feel guilty about it – just acknowledge it and resume your practice.

Reiki self-treatments can both energize and heal you. They also help you to understand energy better.

INANIMATE OBJECTS AND PERSONAL PROBLEMS

Two aspects of working with the First Degree which are perhaps less discussed than the others are working with inanimate objects and with personal problems. The latter get more attention in the Second Degree, but there are ways to work with them at the first level.

Reiki for inanimate objects

People tend to laugh if you mention the idea of giving Reiki to your computer or fridge. But it does work, and it is not that odd if you think back to the explanation of the nature of energy on pages 12–13. Everything originates from the same energy, including the materials used to make a washing machine. They just vibrate at a different rate to animal matter.

If one of your household objects breaks down, put your hands on it and let the Reiki flow. Try not to give it Reiki from an attitude of anger about it having broken; instead send the energy with gratitude for the service it has given you. You should also give the Reiki without expectation of a particular outcome. You may still need to repair or replace an item, but there is healing somewhere in the situation.

When you give Reiki to an inanimate object, send the energy to it with gratitude for the service it has given you.

Write a problem on a piece of paper and use this to send Reiki to the situation with intentions for it to be healed.

Reiki for personal problems

At a meeting after my First Degree class, one of my fellow students told us that she had been trying to sell her house for months but was having no luck. Now, however, she had several potential buyers for the house after going around her house giving Reiki to the walls.

The Reiki teacher told us that even at First Degree level we could give Reiki to issues we were troubled by. One way to do this is to write the problem down on a piece of paper. Once you have done that, hold the paper between your hands and give Reiki to the paper and, therefore, the situation. Be clear and positive in your statement when writing. For example, always write 'I want' rather than 'I don't want'. You must also be open and honest.

If you would like a new relationship to start, don't specify the person you want the relationship with. At the end of my 'wish', I always add these words: 'This or something better now manifests for me in a totally satisfying and harmonious way for the good of all concerned.' Try it yourself and you may be surprised at the positive changes you can make to your life.

GROUNDING YOUR ENERGY

As an energy worker, it is important to know how to ground your energy, and if you are teaching others or giving treatments you should be able to show others how to do it. You should also be able to recognize when others need to be grounded.

One of the symptoms of being ungrounded is a 'spaced out' or dizzy feeling. It can also manifest as a sensation of coming out of the body. This is caused by not being sufficiently connected to earth energy. One way to ground is to stand on grass or earth in bare feet as often as possible. However, after giving a Reiki treatment, or after receiving an attunement (see below), that may not be sufficient.

Attunements

An attunement is a form of spiritual empowerment that passes through the teacher to the student. It activates the student to draw in more energy according to individual need, and enables the student to become a more effective channel for Reiki energy. It can also symbolize the initiation process into a life with Reiki.

Visualization exercise

I use the following exercise for grounding and I also teach it in Reiki classes. Read the instructions through several times. Alternatively, get a friend to read them to you for your first few attempts, or record them, so that you can listen to the instructions. Please don't worry if you cannot 'see' everything as described. That is perfectly normal.

1 Find a straight-backed chair or a stool that allows you to sit with your feet flat on the ground. Remove your shoes, but if it is cold keep your socks on.

2 Close your eyes and breathe deeply three times. Visualize a rope descending from the tail of your spine, through the floor, into the earth, through layers of rock, until you feel it reaches the centre of the earth. Anchor your rope there.

3 Now imagine that there are two holes in the soles of your feet and a heavy, brownish-red sludge is coming up through these holes and circulating throughout your lower body as far up as your waist. Let this energy circulate until your body feels heavier.

4 Next visualize a distant point in the heavens from which a beam of white light is coming down to connect with a point on the crown of your head. Feel this light flow through this point in your head and through the upper part of your body, cleansing it and making it feel lighter.

5 Now feel the two different energies circulating at the same time. Finish by touching the floor with your hands and allowing any excess energy to return to the earth.

PREPARING A SPACE TO TREAT OTHERS

Before treating other people, you need to prepare yourself energetically and prepare your work space. The latter particularly applies if you intend to treat friends and family on a regular basis.

Ideally, you should use a massage table for giving treatments. You can use a bed or a quilt on the floor, but only if you are giving treatments infrequently, otherwise you will end up with back problems. If you are using a table, cover it with a sheet or the paper covers used by massage therapists. You will also need a light blanket to cover the client, as the body becomes cold quickly when relaxed. Also make sure you have a box of tissues near by, as a treatment can be a very emotional experience for some people.

CREATE A RELAXED ATMOSPHERE

If you are working from home, choose the room that you feel will be most relaxing for giving treatments. In an ideal world, you would have a room in the house that can be used for Reiki alone—as this is impossible for many people, select the room that needs the least work to switch it from its everyday function to a room for Reiki.

The most important thing, whatever the circumstances, is that the room is clean, quiet, warm, and comfortable.

Cleansing the room
Air the room well before the treatment and burn some incense before the treatment rather than during it. Some people, especially

It is advisable to burn incense before the treatment begins as some people are irritated by it. Burning oil is a better solution.

A treatment room should be clean, comfortable, quiet, and have been prepared with care and respect for the patient.

those with bronchial problems, are irritated by incense as it tends to give the air a dry quality. Alternatively, you can scent the room with an oil burner, choosing a light oil such as lavender that promotes relaxation.

When preparing a room, another thing to consider is noise. While it can be pleasant to work with a window open in summer, too many sounds from outside can become a distraction for both you and your patient. Similarly, put any nearby telephones on "silent" and use an answering machine.

The right ambience

One sound that does complement a Reiki treatment is that of music. It can be relaxing for both you and your patient and may even influence the success of the treatment. However, make sure you keep the volume at a level where the music can be heard by the client but is not obtrusive. Each practitioner will have his or her own musical preferences, but I like to choose something that is without lyrics, and is melodic, relaxing, and non-energizing all at once. Above all, it should be something that will not disturb the patient.

PREPARING YOURSELF TO TREAT OTHERS

One of the first priorities before giving a treatment is to pay attention to your personal hygiene. Your clothes should be clean, your hands washed, and your teeth brushed. This ensures that no offensive smells, such as those of garlic or tobacco, get in the way of the client's comfort. You should also remove your watch and any jewellery that might get in the way, especially bracelets and rings, although you may keep a wedding ring on if you wish. When I wash my hands just before beginning the treatment, I like to put a tiny drop of rose essential oil on my hands.

The next step is to cleanse yourself energetically. The method that follows is from Chi Kung, but it is remarkably similar to the recently discovered technique used by Japanese Reiki practitioners for removing toxic energy.

MERIDIAN MASSAGE

The intention of this exercise is to cleanse blocked and negative *Ki*. The exercise requires at least six repetitions of the steps, eventually building up to 36. Once you have mastered the technique, you will build up a flowing rhythm that will make this number of repetitions easy to complete. It is not necessary to do this before every single treatment if you are giving several in a day. At the beginning and end of multiple sessions will be sufficient.

Meridian Massage

1 In a standing position, place your left hand on your right shoulder and raise your right arm to shoulder height.

2 Stroke down the outside of your right arm as you swing the arm down and across the front of your body.

3 When your left hand reaches the fingertips, your right hand then strokes up the inside of your left arm to the shoulder as you bring your left arm above your head.

4 When your right hand reaches your left shoulder, sweep it down the outside of your left arm to the fingertips, swinging the arm down at the same time. Now the left hand strokes up the inside of the right arm to the shoulder, which is the position you started at.

ENERGY AND BODY SYSTEMS

Eastern philosophies have detailed explanations
of the movement of energy through the body,
and of the workings of the energy body itself,
all of which add to the Western concept of
body systems.

THE ENERGY BODY

Reiki entails working with the energy body. What I am going to describe in this section is the energy body as it is understood in Chi Kung, as well as the chakra system – because the latter has become the prevalent energetic model in the West. Early Reiki systems focused on working with the *Hara* (see pages 38–39), which is integral to Japanese and Chinese energy work ranging from martial arts to Buddhist meditation.

The aura is an egg-shaped energy shield that surrounds the entire body and that can expand and contract.

The energy body is the one we cannot see, but which, through energy work, we can feel. It surrounds and penetrates every cell of our physical body, vibrating at a higher rate than it. Each person's physical body is unique to them, and has what might be called an energetic signature that is equivalent to the way in which fingerprints provide a unique personal identification.

I discovered Chi Kung some six years after finding Reiki. I was struck by the similarities between the energy I felt while doing Chi Kung exercises and giving Reiki. I mentioned this to my Chi Kung teacher. She agreed there must be similarities, so I asked her why she did not just practise Reiki as it was much simpler. She replied that, while I obviously liked the motorway, she preferred the scenic route. Certainly, much of what I learned through Chi Kung added a new dimension to my Reiki practice, and my understanding of the movement of energy, and the energy body itself.

THE MERIDIANS, CHAKRAS AND AURA

Three elements of the energy body are relevant to Reiki: the meridians (see pages 36–37), the chakras (see pages 40–49) and the aura (see pages 56–59). The first two are different systems of understanding the mechanisms of the energy body, while the aura is common to both. While it is not crucial for the success of a Reiki treatment for the practitioner to have in-depth knowledge of all the meridians, or to know everything about the chakras, it does help to know the location of the physical organs.

SYSTEMS OF THE HUMAN BODY

In this section we will also look at two of the physical human body systems that are of primary importance in healing work: the endocrine system, which corresponds with the chakras, and the nervous system, which is our body's communications centre.

THE MERIDIANS

In Traditional Chinese Medicine (TCM) the meridians are invisible energy channels that run in parallel with the physical anatomical system, but vibrate at a higher rate. Western science, as well as ancient Chinese and Indian scientific systems, suggests that energy vibrating at a higher rate has an effect on matter vibrating at a lower rate. We can deduce from this that if the meridians are adversely affected then the physical body will manifest the symptoms of ill health. The solution is to treat the energy body both by preventing imbalance and by rebalancing it.

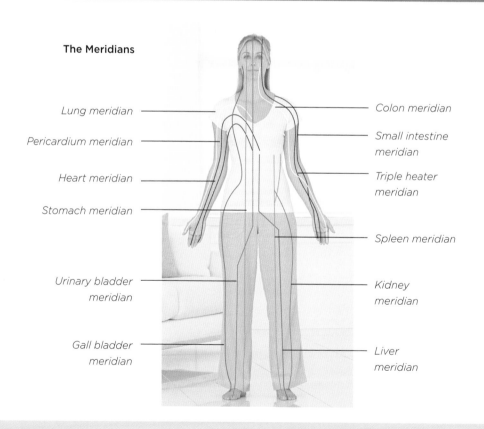

The Meridians

Lung meridian

Pericardium meridian

Heart meridian

Stomach meridian

Urinary bladder meridian

Gall bladder meridian

Colon meridian

Small intestine meridian

Triple heater meridian

Spleen meridian

Kidney meridian

Liver meridian

There are 35 meridians in the Traditional Chinese Medicine system, conducting *Ki* around the body. Within these there are 12 major meridians, 8 extra meridians and 15 collateral channels. It is along the major meridians and the Governor and Conception channels that all the main acupressure points are located. It is useful to know some of these as they can often provide some useful first aid (see pages 96–97).

MAJOR MERIDIANS

The 12 major meridians are each related to a specific organ in the body. They are not 'connected' to the organ itself, but instead to the function of the organ. So, there are heart, lung and kidney meridians, and so on. Each meridian is also linked to the physical and emotional aspects of a person, and they are linked to elements. For example, the stomach meridian is connected with the element of earth, the colour yellow, sympathy, sweetness, flesh and dampness.

ENERGY FLOW

In Traditional Chinese Medicine the flow of energy also follows natural cycles. We are well aware of the effects of the lunar cycle on the body, but less aware of the daily rhythm of the solar cycle. Energy is constantly flowing around your body and the

Body part	Peak energy times
Heart	11 am – 1 pm
Gall bladder	11 pm – 1 am
Small intestine	1 pm – 3 pm
Liver	1 am – 3am
Urinary bladder	3 pm – 5 pm
Lungs	3 am – 5 am
Kidneys	5 pm – 7 pm
Colon	5 am – 7 am
Pericardium	7 pm – 9 pm
Stomach	7 am – 9 am
Triple heater	9 pm – 11 pm
Spleen	9 am – 11 am

flow of *Ki* peaks in each of the 12 major organs for the same two hours every day. For example, between 3 am and 5 am, the flow of *Ki* peaks in your lungs. If you have breathing difficulties you may find that during these hours you are awakened by them as a reaction to the increased energy. See the table above for the peak energy times for the 12 major organs in your body and consider their implications.

THE MICROCOSMIC ORBIT AND ENERGY CENTRES

Circulating *Ki* around the chakras in the body aids healing and increases awareness of the higher self. The two main channels or meridians on which the chakras lie are called the Governor and Conception channels. The Governor (male/Yang) channel runs along the back from the perineum up the spine and over the head and the third eye to the roof of the mouth. The Conception (female/Yin) channel runs along the front from the tongue, through the heart chakra to the perineum. Together they create a circuit called the microcosmic orbit.

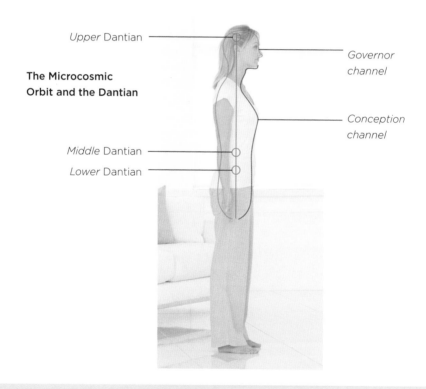

Upper Dantian

The Microcosmic Orbit and the Dantian

Governor *channel*

Conception *channel*

Middle Dantian

Lower Dantian

THE DANTIAN

The focal point of the energy body in Traditional Chinese Medicine consists of the three energy centres, referred to in TCM as the lower, middle and upper *Dantian*. These are linked to the Governor and Conception channels of the meridian system.

Lower Dantian

The *Dantian* of greatest relevance to both Chi Kung and Reiki practitioners is the lower one, which in Japanese is called the *Hara*. This is located just below your navel, and is the storehouse of your energy. This energy is not to be confused with *Ki*, but is the energy that all of us are born with.

Middle Dantian

The middle *Dantian* is just above the navel – sometimes associated with the area around the heart – and is the centre of emotions and of *Ki*.

Upper Dantian

The upper *Dantian* is concerned with our mental and spiritual aspects. It is considered necessary in Chi Kung that you first learn to control the lower centre by grounding the energy there before you start working with the other two. If you don't learn how to ground the energy first, then you may become physically and emotionally unbalanced.

THE THREE TREASURES

At an even more basic level than the meridians and *Dantian* there are the Three Treasures, which are considered to be the foundation of our total composition. They are known as *Jing*, *Chi* and *Shen*.

- *Jing* is our inherited genetic energy and is associated with the lower Dantian or *Hara*. *Jing* is also our sexual energy, which needs to be preserved.

- *Chi* (*Ki*) is the vital essence we depend on for life. The quality of a person's *Chi* depends on the quality of their *Jing*. So, if we strengthen the *Hara*, which will allow us to tap into our *Jing*, we can improve the *Chi* flowing through us.

- *Shen* is our spirit or soul, and this is fed by our *Chi*.

The Three-Treasures system works upwards, with *Jing* feeding *Chi*, and *Chi* feeding *Shen*. We cannot change the *Jing* energy that we were born with, but by working with the *Hara* it can help us to support our *Chi*, which will improve our health and raise our spiritual consciousness.

THE CHAKRA SYSTEM

Chakra is a Sanskrit word meaning 'wheel'. There are seven major chakras in the energy body, with the first situated at the perineum, or base of the spine, and the seventh at the crown of the head. The chakras are traditionally depicted as a lotus flower, which – when combined with the idea of a wheel – results in a circular shape spinning around its centre as the flower petals unfold. Each of the seven chakras has a number of attributes, including a colour, a relation to one of the elements and the maintenance of specific physical and emotional functions.

Chakra	Colour of Influence	Element	Body Sense
Base	Red	Earth	Smell
Sacral	Orange	Water	Taste
Solar plexus	Yellow	Fire	Sight
Heart	Green/pink	Air	Touch
Throat	Turquoise	Ether	Hearing
Brow	Deep blue	Spirit	Extra-sensory perception
Crown	Violet/gold	Spirit	All senses

Most of us cannot see the chakras, but it is possible to become familiar with how they work by focusing attention on their locations and concentrating on how the area feels. Apart from working with energy to influence the chakras, we can work with colour and sound. For example, as each chakra is associated with a specific colour, you can meditate on drawing that colour into the chakra, or wear clothes of that colour to strengthen it. People also work with the sound vibration of each chakra.

The Seven Major Chakras

Crown
(Sahasrara)

Brow
(Anja)

Throat
(Vishudda)

Heart
(Anahata)

Solar plexus
(Manipura)

Sacral
(Svadisthana)

Base
(Muladhara)

CHAKRA 1

The base or root chakra is the first of the seven chakras. Situated at the perineum, between the anus and the genitals, this chakra opens downwards connecting the energy body with the earth. It is associated with security and mental stability as well as survival and prosperity. There are numerous ways to work with this chakra to strengthen it, but at the centre of them all is the importance of connecting with nature and your own sexuality.

CHAKRA FUNCTION

This chakra serves to ground us in the world. The earth energy is pulled upwards through the minor chakras on the soles of the feet, and up the legs, to balance this chakra. If you feel ungrounded, one solution is to take off your shoes and stand on grass or sand, which will help you absorb more earth energy. The energy is then pulled up the spine to balance the testes or ovaries, which are the parts of the endocrine system associated with the root chakra.

Physical health issues

Physical health problems associated with this chakra are ones affecting the feet, ankles and knees, as these are on the route through which the energy flows upwards. Other symptoms of being disconnected from the earth are lower back pain, particularly around the sacrum, and problems with the sexual organs.

Mental and emotional issues

Giving us confidence in ourselves, and in the world, are two of the functions of the base chakra. This chakra can empower you to honour yourself whatever your circumstances. The performance of this chakra throughout our life, if not worked on, is affected by our earliest experiences.

People who were born into a stable environment in which they felt protected will usually grow up feeling that it is safe to trust the world around them. They have little difficulty connecting with the earth energy and are open to receiving it. This keeps their base chakra functioning rather better than if they experienced trauma in the womb, or had an unstable childhood. People experiencing this kind of beginning in life will have a stressed chakra, which then manifests as a lack of trust in the world.

CHAKRA 2

The sacral chakra is physically located just below the navel, in the same location as the *Hara*. The key element of the chakra is water and it is associated with our sexual energy. This refers to our life-sustaining energy rather than the energy we use for sex, which comes from the base chakra. The sacral chakra also has a strong association with the unconscious and with the creative impulse.

CHAKRA FUNCTION

In both Hindu and Taoist teachings, the sexual energy associated with this centre may be transmuted to develop a higher spiritual consciousness by moving the energy up through the higher energy centres. This is not something we all wish to do and, indeed, an attempt to give up sex for the sake of spiritual advancement can result in psychosexual problems.

One of the main functions of the chakra is to help us form healthy emotional and sexual relationships. The energy may also manifest in the form of creativity, and it fuels our enthusiasm and joy in life. Dancing and singing are great activities to strengthen this chakra.

Physical health issues

Physical problems arising from the sacral chakra are connected to the adrenal glands. The adrenals govern how we react to stress. When we are confronted with a stressful situation, adrenalin is released to support our physical and mental ability to cope. However, if the stress is constant, we end up being unable to switch off the flow of adrenalin, and this damages our bodies. The sacral chakra is governed by the element of water; therefore any dysfunction frequently manifests as a disease of the urinary tract and kidneys.

Mental and emotional issues

Dysfunction in this chakra often results in the inability to receive love. This can take the form of being unable to form relationships with the opposite sex. Sex itself may also be unfulfilling, as when the energy tries to rise through the chakras during lovemaking it may not be able to get past the blockages at the second chakra. Unblocked, this chakra enables us to experience unconditional love.

CHAKRA 3

The solar plexus chakra is associated with the Sun and, therefore, connected with the element of fire. It is located at the level of the physical solar plexus, in the centre of the lower ribcage. It is usually associated with personal power, and is the place where we feel 'butterflies in the stomach' when we are in situations that affect our sense of power in both good and bad ways. You can think of this chakra as having the Sun in your body.

CHAKRA FUNCTION

This chakra draws in solar energy, which then enables the flow of energy throughout the physical body. It could be described as an energy hub that feeds energy out along channels called *Nadis*, which are similar to meridians. The last of the chakras before the central heart chakra, it is where we feel power, but also fear and anxiety.

Physical health issues

This chakra is primarily linked to digestion, but is more importantly associated with stress. The connection between digestive problems and stress is commonly seen in ulcers at one extreme, and in simple stomach upsets at the other. Of all the chakras, change in its functioning is perhaps easiest for us to sense because we have all felt the effects of stress in that area. Often what starts as an emotional feeling here quickly becomes physical. Diabetes is also associated with this chakra as it is linked to the pancreas. One of the main ways in which you can strengthen this chakra is to look at stress-reduction techniques. Reiki, used regularly, is perfect for this, and you could add some more physical practices such as yoga or Chi Kung.

Mental and emotional issues

The solar plexus plays an important part in the perception other people have of us. The more energy we are able to draw through this chakra, the more attractive we will seem to other people, as we will be allowing our light to shine (not in an egotistical manner, but as a manifestation of natural self-esteem). Balance in this chakra also enables us to assimilate higher wisdom in our unconscious and access it for our healing. On the negative side, dysfunction in this chakra tends to make us unhappy with life and appear arrogant.

CHAKRA 4

At the centre of the whole system lies the heart. Positioned in the centre of the chest, it is connected to the element of air and is the seat of the higher self. Universally thought of as the place where love originates, this chakra is associated with the qualities of passion and devotion. The heart chakra is not primarily concerned with romantic love, but with generating the energy of an all-encompassing love, such as the love of creation.

CHAKRA FUNCTION

The heart chakra is the gateway between the three lower chakras that are more connected to the physical body, while the three above the heart are more associated with some finer emotions, our spirituality and higher consciousness.

Physical health issues

It is not surprising that this chakra is related to the circulatory system. Heart disease is probably the biggest killer of people in the West, but it is not just a disease created by an affluent lifestyle; it also has a stress component, in that feelings of frustration and anger are as bad for your heart as cholesterol.

We can go a long way to prevent physical heart disease by working to release the issues we hold in our heart chakra, such as emotional trauma, sadness and grief.

Mental and emotional issues

The highest form of love is unconditional love. Even romantic love can be transformed into this if we are able to form meaningful relationships that are respectful of another person's feelings. Perhaps we can only truly love another person in this way by first loving ourselves unconditionally.

Dysfunction of the heart chakra manifests as the inability emotionally to sustain lasting relationships or friendships. If we continue in this state, we eventually 'close down' our whole system, because we will neither give nor receive love.

To support your heart chakra, look for a therapy that will reduce stress and help you to release anger or acknowledge the sadness in your heart. Also, by giving yourself some self-love you will attract love from the Universe.

CHAKRA 5

This chakra is associated with the element of ether and is located between the centre of the collarbone and the larynx. As this is also the location of our vocal cords, it is not surprising that this chakra is primarily associated with our outward communication, and the ways in which we express our inner self.

CHAKRA FUNCTION

The throat chakra acts as a connection between the heart and the head. We often talk about acting from our hearts or our heads, and through the mediation of the throat chakra we express that action. In another sense, you could say it lies between body and spirit. We can use our voice in many ways: to express love, to calm or to give praise. On the other hand, we can use it to express anger and negativity. When we use our voice in this way we create an imbalance in the chakra.

As a healer, you will often be able to hear if a person has an issue in this chakra just by listening to him or her talk. The words he or she uses will obviously give you clues about his or her inner issues, but if you tune into the actual tonal quality of the voice, listening to it as if it was a musical instrument, you will gain a much deeper insight into the person's character.

Physical health issues

Typically, physical ailments associated with dysfunction of this chakra are ear, nose, throat and respiratory problems. As the thyroid gland is also located in this area, hyperthyroidism and hypothyroidism are also indicative of imbalance.

When we have a deficiency in this chakra we become timid, fearful and afraid to speak up, whereas people with an excess of energy here are likely to be loud, and to talk excessively.

Mental and emotional issues

A blockage in this chakra may lead to closing down communications with others. This may lead to depression. People who find it difficult to express their inner feelings verbally may be helped by finding someone who will pay close attention to them, such as a counsellor who has been trained to listen in non-judgementally. The act of talking about problems will help to remove any blocks.

CHAKRA 6

The brow or third eye chakra is located in the centre of the forehead, just above the eyebrows, and like the throat chakra is coupled with the element ether. It is the chakra associated with the mind, and particularly with intuition and psychic abilities. It is also the chakra we draw on when we meditate.

CHAKRA FUNCTION

The mind is the least-understood aspect of the human being. The mind is not simply the brain, as it is so much more than the sum of that organ's parts. This chakra enables us to move beyond the mind as we experience it every day with its constant chatter and movement of thoughts, and tap into the knowledge and wisdom we have within, but of which we are unaware. Dysfunction in this chakra can lead us to become arrogant about having special powers of insight, or psychic abilities, and use them to control other people.

Physical health issues

Physical problems associated with this chakra are ones that affect the head in general, and the eyes. Therefore, headaches and migraines are symptoms of imbalances in this chakra. These can be relieved by strengthening this chakra through quiet meditation to calm the mind and release tension.

Also, most of us overstress our eyes by working long hours in front of a computer. This is another major cause of headaches, and you should try to take your eyes away from the screen as frequently as you can, and if possible look at a plant or gaze out of the window at the sky. The colours of nature and the energy of natural matter are healing in themselves.

Mental and emotional issues

In comparison with the other chakras, the brow chakra is not really linked with emotions as such. However, an imbalance here can strongly affect the pineal gland, which sits in the centre of the brain, directly behind the eyes. This gland is responsible for the production of serotonin and melanin, hormones that affect our mood and our sleep patterns respectively. The pineal gland is light-sensitive; therefore, a lack of light reduces the amount of serotonin released, resulting in seasonal affective disorder (SAD), which often manifests as a depressive state.

CHAKRA 7

The ultimate chakra is directly opposite the base chakra and is located on the crown of the head. Whereas the base chakra faces down towards the earth, the crown chakra opens upwards towards the heavens. It is not associated with any element, and it is the chakra that must not be closed at any time, meaning that healers should be very careful when working around this area.

CHAKRA FUNCTION

The crown chakra connects us to everything that transcends our earthbound state. It is the chakra that keeps us connected to a universal consciousness, and through it we can experience the state of pure being, and of transcendental consciousness.

Physical health issues
As with the brow chakra, dysfunction in the crown chakra can lead to headaches. A tendency to be obsessive is also a mark of imbalance here. Epilepsy is another symptom associated with this chakra. Healers working with people who are suffering from epilepsy should ensure that the person is also receiving medical treatment.

Mental and emotional issues
Denial of life, obsession and the bottling up of anger – also linked to the heart chakra – are connected with the crown. These emotions can result in a physical illness such as high blood pressure, which is associated with the emotion of anger. A degenerative disease, such as Parkinson's, is also linked to dysfunction in this chakra – the symptomatic shaking may indicate a fear of life, and if a person becomes paralyzed he or she is denying life completely, for he or she is unable to move.

The thousand-petalled lotus
The name *Sahasrara* means 'a thousand petals'. The lotus flower is used as a symbol for all seven chakras because the flower itself grows up from the mud and rises through the water to blossom fully in the light. This reflects the human condition of being temporarily earthbound and our physical bodies being composed of earth elements. The water represents our emotions, which we have to work through until we reach the spiritual light represented by the Sun.

Eating foods of a certain colour can help to balance an underactive chakra of the same colour.

THE ENDOCRINE SYSTEM AND CHAKRAS

The function of the endocrine system is to secrete chemicals called hormones throughout the body via the blood-stream, and in doing so to regulate the action of the organs and tissues. Malfunction of the endocrine system leads to a number of problems suggesting imbalance such as diabetes, hyper-thyroidism and infertility, all of which are caused by hormone levels that are either too high or too low.

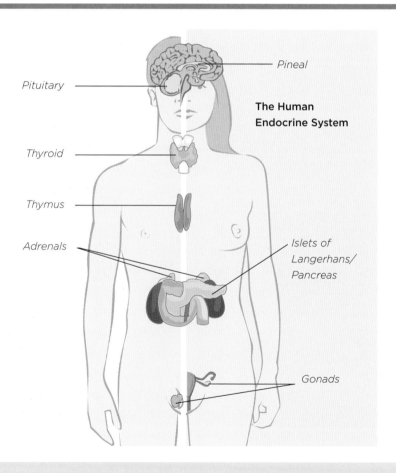

Pineal

Pituitary

The Human Endocrine System

Thyroid

Thymus

Adrenals

Islets of Langerhans/ Pancreas

Gonads

The glands that comprise the endocrine system are:

- The pituitary
- The pineal
- The thyroid and parathyroids
- The thymus
- The Islets of Langerhans in the pancreas
- The adrenals
- The gonads (testes and ovaries)

- The main gland of the endocrine system is the pituitary, which is located in the brain along with the pineal gland. The pituitary coordinates all the other glands and also produces the hormones that influence growth.

- The thyroid gland, in the neck, controls our metabolism. The parathyroids, which are attached to the thyroid, are essential for the maintenance of healthy bones, nerves and muscles, and also balance calcium and phosphorus in the body.

- The thymus, which is situated near the heart, keeps our immune system healthy.

- The islets of Langerhans in the pancreas are responsible for the secretion of insulin and glucogen to maintain correct levels of glucose in the blood. When insufficient insulin is produced, glucose levels rise, resulting in diabetes.

- The adrenals lie just above the kidneys and produce two types of hormones. The outer layer is the source of steroid hormones that balance the salt, sugar and water concentration in the body, while the inner layer supplies adrenalin necessary for stimulating our 'fight-or-flight' reaction to stressful situations.

- The gonads (testes and ovaries) secrete the hormones necessary for reproduction. Women with an imbalance of hormone secretion in the ovaries manifest symptoms varying from infertility to irregular menstruation and pre-menstrual syndrome (PMS).

FAMILIARIZE YOURSELF

As you will see from the diagram on page 53, this system has correspondences with the chakra system. It is therefore important for people engaged in energy work to make themselves familiar with the endocrine system in order to understand various conditions.

Each of the seven chakras corresponds to one or more of the main endocrine glands (see pages 50–51).

The base chakra

The base chakra is linked to the ovaries in women and the testes in men. The ovaries produce the hormones oestrogen and progesterone. Oestrogen is associated with the menstrual cycle, while progesterone is needed to prepare the uterus to receive the fertilized egg. The hormone in the testes is testosterone, which promotes male characteristics and sperm production.

The sacral chakra

The sacral chakra is connected to the adrenal glands that sit above the kidneys and produce adrenalin and cortisol. Adrenalin primes our body to react to stress by raising both the heart rate and blood pressure. Cortisol is our natural anti-inflammatory, and cortisone-based treatments are common in Western medicine for symptoms that include inflammation, such as those associated with arthritis.

The solar plexus chakra

The solar plexus chakra is associated with the Islets of Langerhans, which produce insulin to lower blood-sugar levels and glucogens to raise them. Diabetes and hypoglycaemia stem from malfunctions in this gland.

The heart chakra

The heart chakra is closely linked to the thymus gland, which is the control centre of our immune system, and operates our defence against viral-type infections and airborne germs, such as flu and colds.

The throat chakra

The throat chakra is linked to the thyroid gland, which produces the hormones thyroxine and iodothyronine. These hormones promote human growth and are responsible for cell repair. Thyroid problems can be the result of both a lack of or an excess of these hormones.

The brow chakra

The brow chakra is associated with both the pineal and pituitary glands. The pineal gland secretes both serotonin and melatonin, which are responsible for maintaining mood and sleep patterns. The pineal gland in particular is light-sensitive and is similar in structure to the retina of the eye.

The crown chakra

Like the brow chakra, the crown chakra is associated with both the pineal and pituitary glands. The pituitary gland coordinates all the other glands in the system and as such secretes a number of hormones. Obviously, any problems relating to this gland will have a knock-on effect throughout the whole endocrine system.

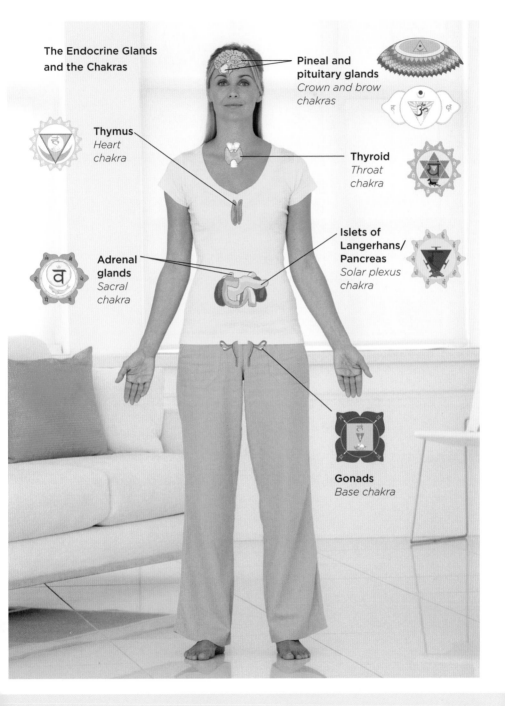

The Endocrine Glands and the Chakras

Pineal and pituitary glands
Crown and brow chakras

Thymus
Heart chakra

Thyroid
Throat chakra

Adrenal glands
Sacral chakra

Islets of Langerhans/ Pancreas
Solar plexus chakra

Gonads
Base chakra

THE NERVOUS SYSTEM

While the endocrine system orchestrates the hormones, the nervous system is the body's control and communications centre. The central nervous system is situated in the brain and spinal cord and controls our conscious and unconscious functions. The peripheral nervous system, consisting of sensory and motor nerves, sends messages to this central system.

Problems associated with the nervous system relate to the brain and include stroke or cerebral haemorrhage. Migraine is another problem, as is meningitis. Psychological problems such as depression, anxiety and insomnia are also associated with the nervous system.

THE AUTONOMIC NERVOUS SYSTEM

All body systems are interconnected so that the body works harmoniously. The system that demonstrates this connection and interdependence, is the autonomic nervous system. This includes part of the peripheral and central nervous system and controls functions that occur without conscious effort.

The autonomic nervous system is composed of two parts: the sympathetic and parasympathetic. These are responsible for regulating heartbeat, blood pressure, breathing rate and body temperature. The sympathetic system deals with involuntary body functions such as breathing. It also activates the adrenal glands in response to stress. The parasympathetic system is most active when the body is in a relaxed state, and it also helps the body recover from a stressful episode.

These two systems need to be in balance to maintain good health. If the sympathetic system is constantly overused, as is often the case in modern living which imposes increasing amounts of stress, it works against our efforts to maintain balance. If we fail to use the parasympathetic system to return to a state of relaxation, it becomes weakened, and (as with unused muscle) it takes time to return to full function. Regular meditation, yoga, Chi Kung and Reiki are all excellent ways of balancing this important body system.

The Human Nervous System

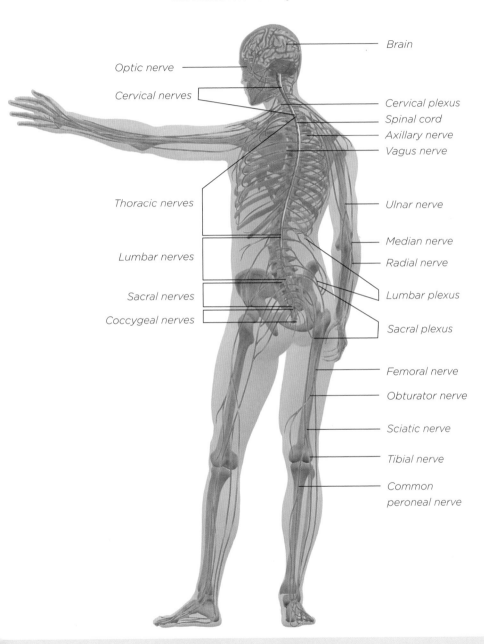

Brain

Optic nerve

Cervical nerves

Cervical plexus

Spinal cord

Axillary nerve

Vagus nerve

Thoracic nerves

Ulnar nerve

Median nerve

Lumbar nerves

Radial nerve

Sacral nerves

Lumbar plexus

Coccygeal nerves

Sacral plexus

Femoral nerve

Obturator nerve

Sciatic nerve

Tibial nerve

Common
peroneal nerve

THE AURA

The final element of the energy body, and the one common to both the meridian and chakra systems, is the aura. The aura is an egg-shaped field of energy that completely surrounds the human body, even extending beneath the feet. It is sometimes described as a 'rainbow of light' as it contains all the colours of the rainbow, as do the chakras (see page 40).

The purpose of this energy field is to support the growth of the physical body, and in this respect it is like an energy grid that exists before the body does. In other words, it may form at the time of conception, although it cannot be detected after death.

Echoing the number of colours in a rainbow, the aura also has seven layers (see page 34). The first layer of energy, closest to the body, has the densest vibrations; these grow successively lighter and faster as the layers get further away from the body. The first layer is red, which is also the colour of the base chakra. The second layer is orange, corresponding with the second chakra, the third is yellow – and so on, with the final layer being the violet associated with the crown chakra. Each of the layers is connected to an aspect of the energy body, as shown in the table on the opposite page.

The aura has long been depicted in religious art, often as a halo. This would seem to indicate that its existence has been recognized for many centuries.

SEEING THE AURA

The aura can be perceived by some people, and clearly many cultures have been aware of its existence for some time, as energy fields around the body and is represented in the visual art of a number of civilizations. In the Western world, the halo is the most common depiction, and is symbolic of the spiritual character of the person.

Interpreting an aura

People who can see auras may have been born with this gift, but it is a skill that can also be developed if worked on. Those who can see auras say that everyone's aura is constantly changing, depending on mood, health and level of spiritual development. The size of a person's aura also changes depending on various circumstances. For example, it can expand to fill a room and touch all the other auras present, or it can be pulled in close to the body, almost like a protective shield.

This expansion and contraction of the aura means that we can pick up and interpret information from the auras of people around us. You may be inexplicably drawn to someone, for example. This probably indicates that there is something in their aura that resonates with you or your own aura. Similarly, your aura may contract close to your body if you sense something that you don't like.

Layer	Colour	Aspect of Energy Body	Quality
1	Red	Etheric body	The five senses
2	Orange	Emotional body	All emotions
3	Yellow	Mental body	Intellectual activity
4	Green	Higher mental body	Interaction with other people, plants, animals; relationships of all kinds
5	Blue	Spiritual body	Connection to the divine
6	Indigo	Causal body	Experience of the spirit world
7	Violet	Ketheric body	Connection to our higher self and our superconsciousness

PRACTISING SENSING THE AURA

There are three simple ways to practise seeing auras. In all of these methods you need to let your eye muscles relax, so that while you are looking directly at the person or plant you are not pulling the eyes into focus with the muscles. Don't expect to see the energy of the aura clearly at first, but relax and allow yourself to get the sense of a shimmer around whatever you are looking at.

Method 1
Sit outdoors and gaze at a plant or a tree that is silhouetted against a plain backdrop, such as a clear sky. All trees have very strong energy fields.

Method 2
Hold your own hand up against the sky and spread your fingers wide. Look between the fingers and concentrate on the outline of your hand.

Method 3
Ask a friend to sit or stand against a white wall. Keep the light dim and observe what you can see around the body.

Method 3

CLEANSING YOUR AURA

You may want to use a smudge stick and feather to cleanse your aura and the healing space (it is easier if someone else can do this for you).

1 Light your smudge stick and have a fireproof bowl filled with sand or earth at hand to extinguish it.

2 Moving the smudge stick around the body, use the feather to disperse the smoke through the aura. This removes any harmful elements in the aura.

REIKI
HAND POSITIONS

The hand positions are integral to all Reiki
practices. They ensure that the healing power
of Reiki is available at all times, and in all places.

HAND POSITIONS FOR SELF-TREATMENT

The simplicity of the system for treating yourself makes it possible for you to self-treat wherever you are. Whether you are travelling or at home, your hands are always available.

Whether you decide to sit or lie down to give yourself a Reiki treatment, always make sure that you are comfortable. If possible, turn off any potential distractions such as your mobile phone.

What follows are the set positions for a self-treatment, and you should follow the order shown here. At times, you may want to deviate from this and concentrate on a specific area. There is nothing wrong with this, although it is always better to treat the whole body as regularly as possible. Similarly, if you don't have time to give yourself a full treatment, you may find that focusing on the kidney area and the head is enough to refresh you.

Beginners often worry about holding the positions for the length of time specified in the instructions. Rather than concern yourself with time, pay more attention to what your hands are telling you and follow them. If your hands feel glued to a spot, keep them in a position as long as you

Giving yourself Reiki every day is one way to show respect for yourself as well as keeping yourself in peak condition. Wherever you are, whatever you are doing, place your hands on yourself and bless yourself with Reiki energy.

are having that sensation. You will probably find that the length of time you take to give yourself a treatment will vary, but as a rule of thumb it should be around 45 minutes.

You may find that if you give yourself a Reiki treatment last thing at night that you will fall asleep before you complete half of the treatment session. This is not a problem and does not affect the benefits Reiki brings you. However, if you want to make sure that you give yourself a full treatment, after waking might be a better alternative.

POSITION 1

Make sure you are in a comfortable position, and that you won't be disturbed before you start treating yourself.

Place your hands over your face with your palms over your eyes and the upper part of your cheeks. Your fingertips should be just above your hairline, and your fingers and thumbs should be close together. Hold the position for at least three minutes.

POSITION 2

This position is a good one to use on its own if you have earache or if you are having problems with your teeth.

Cup your hands over your ears, still keeping your fingers together. Hold the position until you feel ready to move on. If you have toothache, you can also cup your hands over your jaw, fingers together.

POSITION 3

Although this position can be done quite easily sitting up, as seen here, it is easier to do when lying down as there is less strain on the arms.

Cup the back of your head with your hands placed horizontally across the skull. Your fingers will be pointing in opposite directions.

Alternative Position 3
Alternatively, place your hands together, fingers pointing upwards and palms at the base of the skull.

POSITION 4

Keep your left hand on the back of your head in a position that is comfortable for you and does not involve twisting your wrist around. Place your right hand across your forehead, covering it completely.

POSITION 5

There are two versions of this position for treating the throat area. Use whichever you find most comfortable, and again hold the position until you are ready to move on.

Keeping your fingers together, place your left hand around the back of your neck. Then loosely cup your right hand around the front of your throat area, with your thumb pointing towards your right ear. You can reverse this if you wish.

Alternative Position 5

Alternatively, hold this position by cupping both of your hands together in front of your neck, with your fingertips going just behind and under your ears.

POSITIONS 6A AND 6B

These two positions treat the stomach, the spleen and the liver, and are useful on their own if your stomach is feeling upset or if you feel that the spleen and liver need some help in getting rid of body toxins.

Position 6a

For the first body position, place your hands across the solar plexus area, with palms down and fingertips touching in the middle. Remember to keep your fingers together.

Position 6b

When you have finished giving Reiki here, move your hands down, keeping them in the same position, so that your middle fingers are just above your navel, and then give Reiki to this area.

POSITION 7

This position treats the pelvic and reproductive areas organs. It is a good position for women to use to relieve period pain.

Place the heels of your palms on each of your hip bones and point your fingers down and into the middle so that your fingertips touch. You can keep your thumbs in close to your hands or spread them outwards, making a heart shape between your hands.

POSITION 8

The last of the front body positions is one that helps to balance the energy.

Place one hand over the *Hara* or second chakra area, just below the navel, and the other over the fourth chakra, which is beside the physical heart in the centre of the breastbone area.

POSITIONS 9A AND 9B

Clearly, there is no way that you can comfortably treat the whole of your back by yourself. Instead, self-treatment on the back focuses on the kidneys and the adrenals just above the kidneys. For both of these positions, place the palms of your hands on each side of your back with your fingers pointing into your spine. If your back is not very broad your fingertips will touch.

Position 9a

To cover the adrenals, place the outside edge of your hands slightly over the bottom of your ribcage and your hands will naturally be in place.

Position 9b

To cover the kidneys, slide your hands down one hand's width to rest on the lower waist.

POSITION 10

The shoulders are the only other back areas that are reasonably accessible, and as we store so much tension in them it is a good idea to give them Reiki whenever we can. This is a good position to use while you take a break from working on a computer or while you are watching television.

The position can be done in two ways. Cross your arms in front of you and place your hands on the back of each shoulder.

Alternative Position 10

Alternatively, instead of crossing your arms in front of you, put your right hand over the back of your right shoulder and your left hand behind your left shoulder, pointing your fingers towards your spine.

POSITIONS 11 AND 12

These positions are additional and are not taught by the traditional Usui Masters as part of a self-treatment. They can easily be done in the bath or as part of a foot massage or reflexology treatment.

Position 11

The first is giving Reiki to your knees. The knees can hold stagnant energy and fear, as well as being problem areas for people with arthritis and rheumatism. I have included them in the full self-treatment, but they can be done separately. Place your hands on your knees and hold for three minutes.

Position 12

Similarly, your feet and ankles, which do so much hard work, can be treated by simply placing your hands around them in a way that is comfortable.

HAND POSITIONS FOR TREATING OTHERS

Treating others is a privilege and a profound experience in many ways. Using your intuition and listening to your hands is more important than following the hand positions precisely.

A typical Reiki treatment given to another person usually lasts about an hour if each hand position is held for the minimum of three minutes. There are times when you may wish to spend longer on a treatment, perhaps if the person is particularly unwell, you intuitively feel that they need more time in general, or you want to focus on a particular area.

If you are giving a treatment for the first time, you will need to allow extra time before the session begins to discuss the treatment with them and answer any questions they may have.

You may want to allow time for discussion before and after a Reiki treatment.

IMPORTANCE OF THE HEAD

The first five positions are on the head and throat area. I find that with some people I may spend almost half of the treatment time working on the head, especially in the first few treatments.

Since the head is the location of the spirit-centred chakras, the intellect and the main organizers of the endocrine system – the pituitary and pineal glands – it is logical that this area requires extra attention. However, it varies according to the needs of each recipient.

FLOWING MOVEMENTS

Regular practice at giving treatments to others will ensure that the transition between hand positions is smooth. Having self-confidence and controlling your breathing will help to make your movements flow. This makes for a more relaxing experience for you both.

POSITIONS 1A AND 1B

These positions help you to tune into another person's energy flow.

Position 1a

Have the recipient lie comfortably on their back on the treatment table, hands by their sides, not folded over the stomach, and seat yourself behind their head. As a starting point, rest your hands gently on their shoulders for a few moments. This helps you to tune into their energy flow.

Position 1b

Place your hands together, with the sides of your thumbs touching and palms down, just above the recipient's face. Slowly lower your hands onto the face. Ensure that your thumbs are placed in the middle of the forehead and slightly over the top of the bridge of the nose. Place your palms over the eyes and lightly rest your fingers on the cheeks. Hold for three minutes.

POSITIONS 2A AND 2B

There are variations on some of the positions, depending on the preference of the Master. Shown here are two variations on the second position, both of which were taught to me by Masters of the traditional school.

Position 2a

Place the palms of your hands over each of the recipient's ears, with your thumbs in front of the ears. Your fingers should fall into a natural position over the back of the jaw and neck.

Position 2b

Place the heel of your palm above each temple with your palms over the temples. Your fingers should lie against the side of the face, with the little fingers resting in front of each ear.

POSITIONS 3A, 3B, AND 3C

It takes some practice to manoeuvre your hands gracefully into these positions. Breathe into your centre and don't rush it at any point. Many recipients feel tense when you are manoeuvring them into this position and are unable to allow you to fully support their head and neck. Encourage them to let you take the weight of their head, but don't mention it too many times or they will become more self-conscious.

Relaxed or not, this is a favourite position for many people, probably because it echoes the way a mother holds a baby's head. After a treatment, some people have singled out this position as the one that makes them feel 'very cared for'.

Position 3a
Slide your right hand from over the recipient's ear onto the side of their cheek. Place your left hand on the left side of the recipient's face and slowly guide the head over to the right, so that the back of your right hand is now touching the table.

Position 3b

Now place your left hand under the back of the head with your fingers pointing down and over part of the neck.

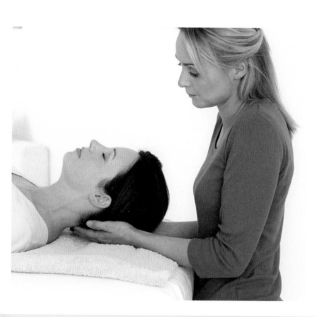

Position 3c

Slowly roll the recipient's head over to the left so that the back of your left hand is touching the table and their head is supported in your left palm. Bring your right hand in under the back of the head so that your hands are cradling the head and the top of the neck. Make sure your hands are comfortable and that the recipient's head feels secure and well balanced.

POSITIONS 4A AND 4B

Moving gently out of position 3 when performing 4a and 4b.

Position 4a

Slide one hand into the centre back of the recipient's head. When you have the head supported, remove your other hand from the back of the head and place it, with closed fingers, over the forehead. The fingers should be pointing sideways so that your hand is lying across the forehead.

Position 4b

After holding position 4a for 3–5 minutes, first remove your hand from the forehead and slip it back under the neck. This provides support while you slowly slide your other hand out from under the head, pulling your hand towards you.

POSITIONS 5A AND 5B

Some people find it uncomfortable to have another person's hands too close to their throat, and you should consider this when deciding how to treat this area. Also remember that the throat is an area that holds an enormous amount of emotional issues for many people, and during treatment some very strong images, emotions and even pain can surface.

Position 5a

First rest your elbows on either side of the recipient's head (but not too close) and bring your hands in front of the throat area, approximately 7.5 cm (3 in) away from the throat. Interlace your fingers with the tips of your thumbs just touching (it doesn't matter if they don't) and cup the jawline and throat area. There are variations on this position. Simply lay your hands on each side of the recipient's jaw with your thumbs just above the jawbone and your fingers pointing towards each other, but not interlaced. This version brings your hands closer to the throat area, while in the position shown your hands should be kept some distance from the throat.

Position 5b

Finish by unlacing your fingers and pulling your arms away in an arc until they reach the edge of the table.

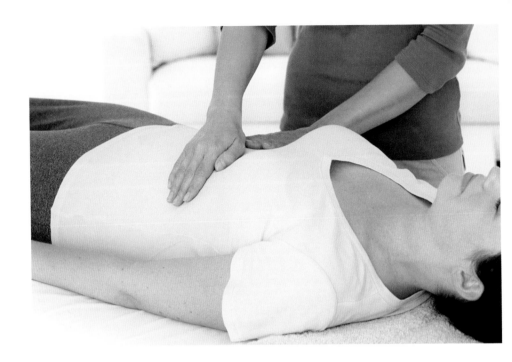

POSITION 6

Having finished the recipient's head and throat area, you move on to treat the rest of the front of their body. In order to do these positions, you will need to stand up unless you have the type of office chair that moves around on castors.

For the first body position, place your hands one behind the other beneath the chest area (on a woman, just below the breasts), across the ribs. Hold the position for three minutes.

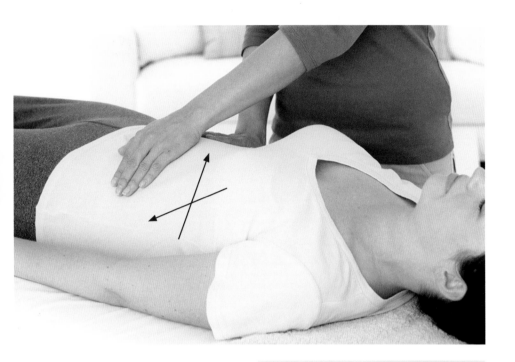

POSITION 7

Use the version of this position that feels most appropriate. What is important with both methods is that you cover the chakras and major organs.

To move from Position 6 into this position, you can either keep your hands in the same place and simply slide them 2.5–5 cm (1–2 in) down the recipient's body, or you can slide the hand farthest from you towards you and down the body, while sliding the hand nearest to you across to the other side. You can use this crisscross motion on the back of the body as well as the front.

Alternative Positions 6 and 7

An alternative way to do the sixth and seventh positions is to start by placing your hands together on one side of the recipient's body, holding the position for three minutes, then slide both your hands over to the other side of the body.

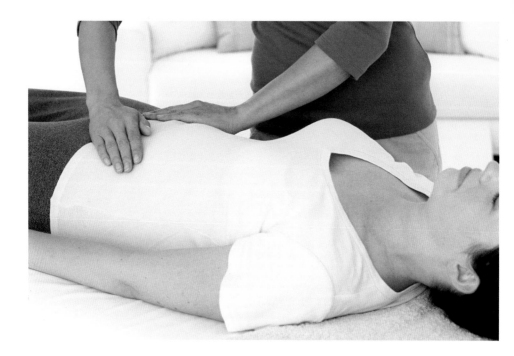

POSITION 8

This position treats the pelvic area. As you are working near the genitals, you will need to show sensitivity and avoid any direct contact with the genitals themselves. The position shown here is most suitable for working with women.

Place your left hand on the inner side of the recipient's right hip bone, fingers together and pointing down towards the pubic bone. Then place the heel of your right hand a small distance from your left fingertips, pointing your hand upwards on the inner side of the left hip bone so that your hands are making a V-shape.

Alternative Position 8 for working with men

Instead of placing your hands in a V-shape across the pelvic area, it is better to place a hand on, or just inside each hip bone. The easiest way to do this is to place one hand with the fingers facing straight up, and place the other with the fingers facing down. Being careful in this area will avoid any embarrassment on either you or your client's part.

POSITION 9

This position concludes treating the front of the body by balancing and linking the energy in the upper and lower sections. This position works with the sacral and heart chakras.

Place your right hand on the recipient's abdomen and your left hand on the breastbone, fingers pointing to the head. Stay in this position for 3-5 minutes or until you feel the energy is in balance between your hands.

POSITIONS 10 AND 11

Use these positions if you feel they are appropriate to the needs of the recipient, or use them to find out the sequence of treatment positions that you think works best for most recipients.

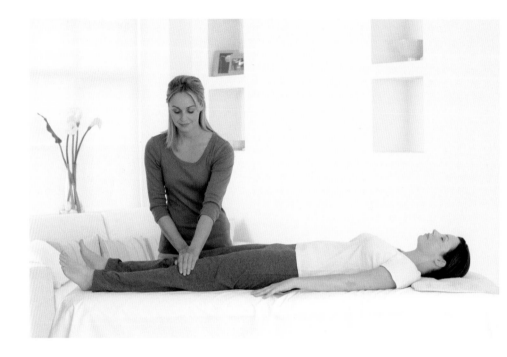

Position 10

The first position treats the knees. You move from the pelvic position to this position, one hand at a time. Hold the position for three minutes.

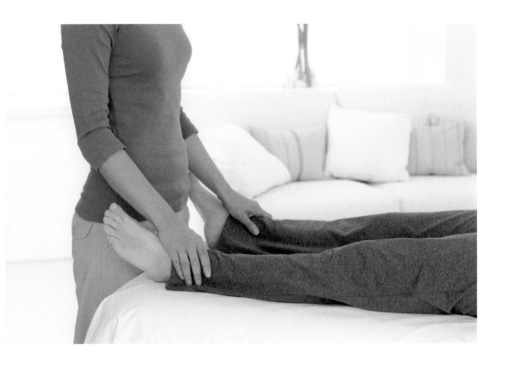

Position 11

Stand at the bottom of the table and move your hands down to the ankles and feet, holding them with your hands pointing upwards. Next ask the recipient to turn over onto their stomach. As most recipients are very relaxed by now, tell them to turn over slowly. You can arrange their hands by their sides, although some people prefer to rest their head on their arms. This is fine, but it does make it more difficult for you to do the first back position, as their muscles are scrunched up. One solution is to ask the recipient to keep their arms by their sides just while you carry out the first position.

POSITION 12

The shoulders hold a lot of tension for most people. Some recipients' shoulders feel like sponges, soaking up energy, and you may find that your hands don't want to move. This feeling of your hands being glued into a position can occur at any time during a Reiki treatment, so it is best just to stay in the position until your hands feel ready to move, as that area of the body obviously needs extra energy.

This position is also a good one to use on its own with the person seated. For example, if one of your family has been working at a computer for long hours, you can encourage them to take a break and give them ten minutes of Reiki on the shoulders and back of the neck. You can also combine this position with giving a head massage.

Lay your hands across the recipient's shoulders, in the same way as on the front of their body. I find it slightly easier on my hands in a straight line, but instead allow them to curve a little so that one hand is pointing slightly upwards and the other downwards.

POSITION 13

Treating the back of the heart area may produce some interesting sensations and you might feel inclined to spend more time here than usual when treating some people. As everyone is unique and you never know in advance what you might feel, listen with your hands at all times.

Move your hands from the recipient's shoulders down to the back of the heart area and hold for three minutes. This is an area that may require some extra attention. You are also covering the lungs at this point, so it is worth spending some more time here if necessary. You may find that you sense different emotional responses in the recipient around the heart area. Sometimes they will be aware of these and mention them, while with other people you alone may feel what is going on. Depending on the length of a person's back, you may be able to fit in another hand position over the area just below the heart, before then moving on to the adrenals and the kidneys.

POSITION 14

To cover the adrenals and kidneys completely, you will probably need to do this position in stages.

Move your hands down the recipient's back from the previous position, first covering their adrenals, and then move your hands down again and cover their kidneys. If the recipient has back pain around the tail end of the spine, you may want to keep moving your hands down until you have covered the whole area. If your recipient is male, you can treat the prostate gland by placing one of your hands on top of the other in the centre of his buttocks, just below the tailbone, after you have completed the back sessions.

POSITION 15

This final position grounds the recipient and needs to be done in two stages, treating each side of the body in turn.

Some people, myself included at times, experience quite dramatic sensations with this position. I remember receiving treatments where I felt that I had expanded to fill the room, and it was only when the practitioner got to this position that I felt as if I was filling my 'normal' space again. Similarly, if I felt my energy was unbalanced during a treatment in terms of right and left sides, this position equalized it again.

Position 15a
Place one of your hands at the top of the recipient's leg nearest to you and place your other hand flat against the sole of their foot. Hold this position for three minutes.

Position 15b
Stand at the other side of the table to treat the other leg. When I move around the bottom of the table to get to the other side, I hold onto one of the recipient's feet so that contact is not lost. Repeat the position on the recipient's other leg and foot. It is possible to lean across the table to do both stages of this position, provided you don't find it puts strain on your back.

CLEARING THE AURA

Now that you have finished the treatment, all that remains is to clear the aura and help the recipient to feel grounded before she gets up. Smoothing down an aura after a treatment helps the energy to settle down and can also remove any negative energy. There are many ways to clear the aura and I have tried several of them. Shown here is the method of the traditional school.

SMOOTHING DOWN THE AURA

The method I use starts on the physical body itself, finishing off by working in the outer layers of the aura.

Place your hands on the sides of the recipient's hips and pull firmly down to their feet. Shake off the excess energy from your hands. Do this three times.

Then place your hands on their back, around the waist area. Push your hands up towards the heart, outwards over each shoulder and down the outside of the arms. Shake off the excess energy from your hands. Do this three times.

Now, working with your hands about 30 cm (1 ft) away from the body, smooth off the aura itself. Start at the crown of the head and work down to the feet.

FINISHING OFF

Having smoothed down the aura, I place my hand in the centre of the recipient's back and gently rub it in a circular motion. Sometimes I also say their name softly if they are having trouble coming round. The more relaxed a person is during the treatment, the longer it takes to rouse them. When you have done this, you can then bring water to the recipient. You should advise them to drink as much water as possible for the next day or two, as this will help to remove toxins more rapidly.

Once the recipient has roused, I leave the room quietly so that they can get up in their own time (but with an elderly person, or somebody with balance or back problems, it is best to stay and help them get up from the treatment table). I then wash my hands to finish the session symbolically and clear myself of any of the recipient's energy.

TALKING ABOUT THE TREATMENT

Most clients either want to relate their experiences during the treatment, or ask what you felt. They want to know if you could feel blockages in their body, and whether you can tell if there is anything wrong. This is when you need to exercise caution and sensitivity. It is not easy to interpret energy sensations as they don't always mean the same thing. My interpretation of a cold sensation around the kidneys might be completely different to another practitioner's. Added to this, the meaning of a sensation I feel in one client may have an entirely different meaning in another client.

Do not make any diagnosis, but talk in general terms about what they felt in different areas of the body and whether they have had any problems there before. In this way, you guide them towards their own conclusions.

PATTERNS OF HEALING

Responses following a treatment vary from person to person. Some people experience an incredible burst of physical energy, while others feel the need to go home and sleep. As a practitioner, you should not take this as an indication that the treatment was not successful. This is simply the response of that person on that particular occasion. You can explain to them that we all have different responses, although you cannot explain to them why they happened to have that experience.

If the person appears to be a bit 'spaced out' or dizzy after the treatment, make sure that they are grounded before they leave. This is especially necessary if they are going to drive straight away. You can do this using part of the grounding exercise on pages 26–27. Get them to sit with their feet flat on the floor and visualize the energy pouring out through the soles of their feet into the ground.

HOW MANY TREATMENTS?

The next thing to consider is the number of treatments a person needs. This very much depends on the condition that is being treated. Reiki can be used to treat both acute and chronic conditions. An acute condition is one that is temporary, such as cuts, colds and viral infections. Headaches are also acute

It is important to ensure that a person is grounded after a treatment and that they do not leave without feeling 'earthed'.

unless they are frequent, in which case they are a sign of an underlying chronic condition. Chronic conditions are long-term ones, such as arthritis. However, many chronic conditions also have acute episodes, asthma and eczema being two typical examples.

Acute conditions

These may respond well after only one or two treatments. I used to suffer from flu regularly and found it very difficult to recover every time. Just before I learnt Reiki, I caught yet another bout of flu and asked a friend who had just become a Reiki practitioner if she would give me a treatment. As she gave me Reiki, I felt my body become heavier and heavier until I felt as if I had turned into a block of concrete. This sensation was followed by one of this heaviness flowing into the floor I was lying on. When the treatment had finished, I expected to feel a little better. However, the flu had gone in that one session, and I felt even better than before I had become ill.

You will probably find that with an acute condition, such as a cold or flu, the best approach is to give treatments frequently within a relatively short period. This is easier to do with a family member than it is with clients attending a Reiki practice, as you are on hand at home to give treatments as often as needed. Always give a full treatment every time, and if required extra treatment on specific areas.

Chronic conditions

These require a longer-term approach. The root causes of a chronic condition form at the level of mind and spirit before manifesting as physical symptoms. For example, the causes of chronic conditions appearing in later life have been forming for some time. Therefore it is unlikely that the causes can be removed quickly.

It is impossible to say exactly how many treatments a person with a chronic condition will need, but it is responsible to advise them that they will probably require many treatments. Ultimately it is their decision to continue or stop treatments, so one way to approach the query is to suggest they have some treatments and see how they get on with them.

With chronic conditions, it is often a good idea to tell the person being treated that sometimes a condition gets worse before it gets better. Everyone has their own healing pattern, and while people often feel some immediate relief after the first treatment they may find that after the next few treatments their symptoms get worse. This is discouraging for them and they may wish to give up. It is then helpful for them to know that others have similar experiences, and that staying with the Reiki, perhaps supplemented with other therapies, will take them through the healing crisis.

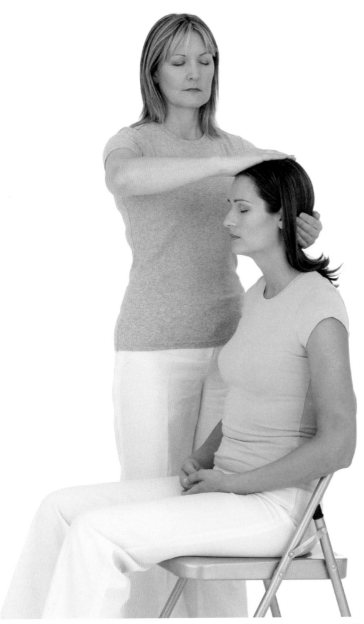

The number of treatments needed depends on the nature of the condition being treated.

REIKI FOR
COMMON CONDITIONS

The following pages present a number of
common conditions and instruction for using
the Reiki hand positions to alleviate some or all
of the symptoms.

REIKI FIRST AID

In general, Reiki has not been taught in the West as a method of treating specific conditions. Instead it is a treatment for all conditions, and the practitioner takes the same approach with every recipient, whatever problem they have. However, there has always been some acknowledgement in classes that Reiki can be used effectively when a person has an accident, and when a full Reiki treatment would not be possible.

You can use the Reiki hand positions to focus on specific areas of the body.

For example, if you have a headache it might be in your best interests to give yourself a full self-treatment, but it is not always necessary as you can just treat the head area. This applies to treating others for the same problem. Similarly, cuts, burns, bites and shock can be treated by focusing on the injured site immediately after the accident has happened.

This section looks at treatments for specific common conditions. These are not intended to replace full body treatments but to offer hand positions for focusing on the relevant areas of the body. Conditions such as anaemia, high blood pressure and others that are longer-term conditions and as such not strictly speaking ´first aid´ are included here because self-treatment of specific points may help you when the condition appears to be worse than normal, or you have an acute flare-up. If you do have a chronic condition, regular, full body treatments are advised, but there may be times when you are not able to do this and simply want to ease the symptoms at work, when travelling or in other similar situations.

CAUTION

Although it is the nature of Reiki to never cause harm to the receiver, it is advisable to be aware that some conditions require caution. This section of the book is not intended as a substitute for medical advice. While the advice and information are believed to be accurate and true, the reader should consult a physician in all matters relating to health and particularly in respect of any symptoms that may require diagnosis or medical attention. Reiki practitioners are not qualified to diagnose conditions, nor should they do so.

Complementary Therapies

Throughout this section you will also find suggestions for the use of complementary therapies that can be applied alongside Reiki, and which feature in Chapter 5.

SHOCK

Shock causes a sudden reduction of the supply of blood to the vital organs, such as the heart, lungs and brain. Shock can be an emotional response to bad news or to seeing a highly disturbing event, or part of the response to a sudden accident, in which case there will be both a physical and a mental element. The body can also physically go into shock as a result of severe dehydration through diarrhoea. Symptoms include clammy and pale skin, shallow and rapid breathing, dizziness, anxiety, nausea, vomiting, coldness and shaking.

Physical shock is a part of some allergic reactions. For example, an allergic reaction, at its most extreme, makes people go into 'anaphylactic' shock. Most commonly, this is caused by eating nuts, and by bee or wasp stings. People who have this level of allergic reaction should carry anti-histamine in a hypodermic syringe with them at all times, as they need to be treated within minutes.

Complementary treatments

- **Aromatherapy oils** such as lavender, melissa or peppermint may be dropped on a handkerchief and held under the nose until the condition eases or until medical help arrives.

- **Bach flower remedies** Rescue Remedy is part of many first-aid boxes. You can either put 4 drops in 30 ml of water and drink it, or dab it on the temples and wrists to reduce symptoms.

REIKI TREATMENT

The symptoms of shock can appear frightening. Try to remain calm and in control as you give a treatment.

To bring a person out of a state of shock, place your hands on the solar plexus and heart areas. You can place both hands on the front at the same time, or on the back. Often it may be more comforting to treat front and back simultaneously. However, depending on the situation, you will have to adopt whatever position you can get to at the time.

HIGH BLOOD PRESSURE

Blood pressure is the measurement of the force of the flow of blood through the arteries. When the pressure is abnormally high, it leads to a condition called hypertension. This condition increases the risk of heart attack and stroke. Hypertension is caused by a number of different factors, such as a family history of it, stress, alcohol consumption, smoking and diabetes, and it can occur during pregnancy. Symptoms include dizziness, headaches, fainting and visual disturbance.

High blood pressure can also have emotional causes. When emotions – especially anger, frustration and grief – are repressed, they build up force internally, and if not released will threaten to explode at some point. Often when anger is expressed in this situation it is with such force that it drives the blood pressure up. This can be seen in reddening of the face.

Complementary treatments

- **Aromatherapy oils** that have calming properties are helpful. Lavender is a good choice.

- **Bach flower remedies** Use remedies for the specific emotions being experienced.

- **Diet** Reduce intake of red meat, fats and salt.

- **Exercise** Non-competitive exercise, such as walking, swimming, yoga or Chi Kung, is excellent for lowering blood pressure naturally.

- **Meditating** on a regular basis, including visualizations that calm the mind, is beneficial.

REIKI TREATMENT

The positions for treating high blood pressure are similar to those for treating anger as they may originate in similar areas of the body, such as the adrenals.

1 Place your hands over the thyroid area of the throat using Position 5. This will help emotional expression.

2 Treat the adrenals and kidneys using Position 14.

3 Place one hand across the back of the head and the other hand on the side of the neck to cover the major carotid artery.

4 Place one hand on the heart and the other on the solar plexus.

CIRCULATORY PROBLEMS

Problems with the circulation of blood around the body can be acquired, and in many cases people are born with what is usually referred to as 'poor circulation'. It is diagnosed as a condition in which the veins and arteries don't carry the blood around efficiently.

Typical causes of this condition are hypertension, high cholesterol, excessive alcohol and smoking, as well as diabetes. In orthodox medicine, it tends to be treated by a combination of exercise, diet modification, and in some cases medication. Emotional aspects of the condition may have roots in an unwillingness to be in the flow of life. For example, if you have poor circulation in your legs and feet, you may unconsciously not want to go in the direction your life is taking you.

Complementary treatments

- **Acupuncture** This is useful for stimulating the heart and spleen.

- **Diet** As with hypertension, circulatory problems benefit from a reduction in consumption of foods that are fatty and high in cholesterol.

- **Exercise** Walking and swimming are perfect activities for stimulating the circulation and detoxifying the system.

REIKI TREATMENT

Steps 1-3 can be used for self-treatment. Steps 4 and 5 can only be used on others.

1 Place your hands over the spleen, on the left side of the body, covering the lower ribcage and waist area, using the alternative to Positions 6 and 7.

2 Then place your hands over the heart and solar plexus.

3 Place your hands in a V-shape on the tops of the legs with the fingers pointing away from you.

4 Place one hand on the shoulder and another on the wrist. Allow the energy to run up and down the arm. Repeat on the other side.

5 Finally, place one hand just below the buttock and the other on the sole of the foot, using Position 15. Repeat this on the other leg.

ANAEMIA

Anaemia occurs when the production and functioning of red blood cells is affected detrimentally. Red blood cells are produced in our bone marrow and are necessary for carrying oxygen around the blood. The most common form of anaemia is caused by iron deficiency.

The other types of anaemia are aplastic anaemia, which is caused by very low production of red blood cells, and megablastic anaemia, which is caused by vitamin deficiency. Symptoms include fatigue, headache, dizziness and palpitations. Emotional aspects of the condition include unexpressed anger and fear.

Those most at risk of anaemia are the elderly, pregnant women and children with an unbalanced diet. Treatment is usually iron supplements and Vitamin B12, while more serious cases may require transfusions.

Complementary treatments

- **Aromatherapy massage** This (or any other therapy that increases feelings of self-worth and love) will help.

- **Diet** This is an important aid to treating this condition. The more iron you can take in naturally, the better. This is found in some fish, egg yolks and dark green, leafy vegetables such as spinach and broccoli. Foods rich in vitamins B12, C and E are essential for the absorption of iron. Avoid dairy products, caffeine drinks and tea, which interfere with iron absorption.

- **Exercise** Yoga or Chi Kung will improve liver function and general well-being.

REIKI TREATMENT

The focus of a Reiki treatment for anaemia is on the liver, as this is the organ that metabolizes iron. The liver is a hard-working organ and deserves as much treatment as you can give it, as it is so important for many other functions of the body.

1 Treat the liver using Position 7.

2 Then place your hands over the heart, also covering the area of the thymus gland.

3 Place one hand over the thymus, and the other hand over the spleen. This helps to build the immune system and purify the blood.

BLOOD CHOLESTEROL

Cholesterol is a fat produced by the liver, or absorbed from foods that are high in cholesterol, such as dairy products. Cholesterol is used in the manufacture of hormones and is an important component of cells. However, although it is important, orthodox medicine states that a level of cholesterol above 160 mg/dl is dangerous for us, and that it is a leading cause of heart attack and stroke. Apart from our diet, diabetes and a hereditary disposition can raise cholesterol levels.

High cholesterol produces no symptoms; therefore the only way we have of knowing our level is to have it measured. It used to be the case that this required a visit to the doctor, but now testing kits can be bought at most chemists, so that you can monitor it yourself. Dietary changes are usually enough to reduce the level. Emotional causes are a lack of joy in life and a very rigid way of thinking. Stress can also be a cause of high cholesterol.

Complementary treatments

- **Diet** As mentioned above, this plays a crucial part. Including more wholegrains such as oats and barley will help, as will either eating plenty of garlic or taking a good garlic supplement.

- **Massage and aromatherapy massage** These will reduce stress and treat the emotions.

- **Meditation** Meditating regularly to reduce stress will lower cholesterol levels.

REIKI TREATMENT

These positions focus on organs associated with the digestive system and our metabolism of food. It is also aimed at improving our emotional attitude to life.

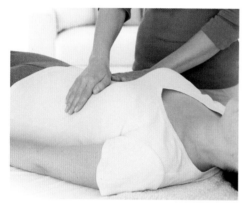

1 Place your hands across the upper ribcage using Position 6. This will treat the stomach.

2 Move your hands down one position to cover the liver, using position 7.

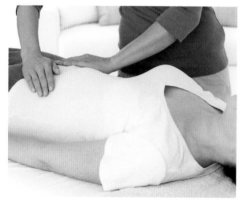

3 Place your hands down further to cover the spleen and colon, using Position 8.

4 Place your hands over the heart and solar plexus to increase the feeling of joy in life.

DIABETES

Diabetes is an increasingly common condition. Although it is very treatable, people need to be aware that this is a serious, sometimes life-threatening condition. It can also lead to a number of other serious conditions such as retinopathy, which can result in loss of eyesight. The fact that diabetics have increased in number points to some imbalance in the well-being of the general population, with diet and stress being the main culprits.

There are two types of diabetes. Type 1 is insulin-dependent diabetes, and arises when the pancreas produces little or no insulin. This type of diabetes is treated with daily shots of insulin and careful attention to diet and eating schedules.

When a young person is diagnosed with diabetes, it is more likely to be this type. Type 2 diabetes occurs when the pancreas only produces a minimal amount of insulin. This type of diabetes can be treated with diet and exercise and tends to be caused by obesity and age.

Emotionally, people with diabetes may not be able to enjoy any sweetness in their lives, by giving love either to others or to themselves. They also have problems releasing stress, which is why the adrenals, liver and pancreas can become overworked.

Complementary treatments

- **Acupuncture** Treatment to support the liver and the adrenal glands will help.

- **Diet** Include more wholegrains and fruits, green vegetables, pulses and garlic. Avoid foods with animal fat, dairy products and sugar.

- **Exercise** Walk every day for 20–30 minutes, or attend a yoga or Chi Kung class every week – both offer exercises to strengthen the internal organs.

REIKI TREATMENT

When there is no time for a full treatment, or it is impractical, these two positions will act as first aid for the physical and emotional aspects of diabetes.

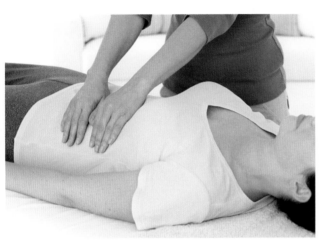

1 Treat the pancreas and liver with the hands placed one above the other as in alternative Position 6 and 7 but on the right side of the body.

2 Treat the adrenals and kidneys using Position 14.

GALLBLADDER DISEASE

The gallbladder plays an important part in the digestive system, as it secretes enzymes and chemicals that enable us to digest our food. The most common symptom of problems with the gallbladder is the formation of gallstones, which cause enormous pain as they pass out of the gallbladder into the bile duct. The gallbladder may also become inflamed owing to the gallstones blocking the outlet.

Apart from the pain of gallstones, other symptoms of gallbladder disease are headaches, fevers and chills, along with irritability and being quick to lose your temper. Causes of the disease are a diet high in fats and cholesterol. Reducing these in the diet restores the gallbladder function and gallstones can dissolve naturally, although in some cases surgery is necessary to remove gallstones.

Emotional causes relate to the function of bile in the gallbladder. Bile has long been thought to represent bitterness and resentment. If you can learn forgiveness, you will reverse the negative emotions and their effects.

Complementary treatments

- **Acupressure and acupuncture** Both are helpful to stimulate the liver and gallbladder meridians.

- **Diet** Avoid meat, eggs, nuts and nut-based products, sugar, alcohol and dairy products. Increase your consumption of olive oil and juices such as apple, beetroot and carrot.

- **Exercise** Chi Kung offers exercises to strengthen the liver and gallbladder meridians, which you can do at home by yourself.

REIKI TREATMENT

On the front of the body, work your way down from below the breastbone to the hip bone placing your hands across the body. This will probably take three steps.

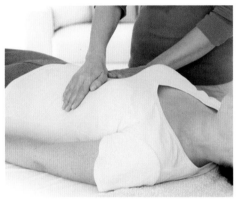

1 Treat the liver using Position 6.

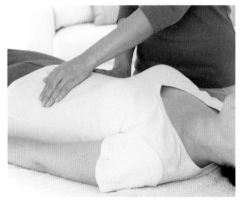

2 Move into Position 7 or alternative position 6 to treat the spleen.

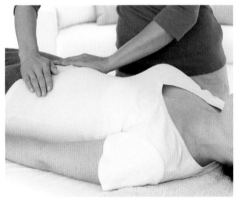

3 Place your hands on the abdomen in a V shape to treat the intestines, using Position 8.

4 Finally, treat the adrenals and kidneys using Position 14.

TOOTHACHE AND GUM DISEASE

Toothache occurs at all ages. Most toothache is the result of tooth decay, inflammation of the pulp of the tooth, neuralgia or a dental abscess. It can also be caused by gingivitis, which affects the gums, or infected sinuses, in which case the person experiences what is known as referred pain.

The pain can be a continuous throbbing or intermittent, and may be caused by eating something that irritates the exposed nerve of the tooth. In many cases, it is caused by infection of the root nerve or the pulp. Tooth and gum disease is caused by poor dental hygiene and a diet that is high in sugar, fat and animal protein. A deeper-rooted emotional cause of the condition is thought to be an internal conflict over what we are saying to the outside world about ourselves. The teeth represent our foundations and feeling insecure may lead to problems with teeth and gums.

Severe toothache or an abscess on the tooth will usually require urgent dental treatment, but in all cases you can help relieve the symptoms with Reiki and some other treatments.

Complementary treatments

- **Acupuncture** Treatments to stimulate the liver meridian will help to relieve and prevent dental problems.

- **Aromatherapy** Tea tree oil, regularly massaged into the gums, will help to prevent infection.

- **Bach flower remedies** Rescue Remedy can be dabbed onto the infected tooth.

REIKI TREATMENT

Toothache is one of the worst pains that we can experience. These positions alleviate acute pain, and the heat of your hands alone will feel soothing to the recipient.

2 Move your hands into Position 5. Remember that this position is different for self-treatment.

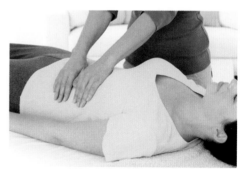

1 Cup the recipient's jaw in your hands with your thumbs tucked under the jawbone. This will treat the entire area.

3 Place your hands over the liver area on the right side of the body, using alternative Position 6 and Position 7.

THYROID DISORDERS

The thyroid gland regulates our metabolism and our levels of energy. Thyroid disorders come in two forms: hyperthyroidism and hypothyroidism. A person with hyperthyroidism may experience weight loss, fatigue, anxiety, palpitations and sensitivity to heat. Someone with hypothyroidism will experience weight gain, tiredness, dry skin and sensitivity to cold.

Emotionally, people with hypothyroidism may feel defeated and depressed by the process of living; those with hyperthyroidism have a stressed, nervous attitude.

REIKI TREATMENT

These positions strengthen both the thyroid gland and the base chakra.

Complementary treatments

- **Diet** Eat iodine-rich foods such as seaweed, raw vegetables, pulses and wholegrains.

- **Rebirthing** This technique should be done with a trained therapist, but can be helpful in clearing the emotions behind this condition.

1 Treat the thyroid area using any hand position that feels comfortable to you. You can use Position 5.

2 Treat the base chakra, using Position 8 or by placing your hands over the base chakra if you are self-treating.

ARTHRITIS

Arthritis is an inflammation of the joints and has a number of forms. The four main ones are: osteoarthritis, which is a consequence of wear and tear on the joints and is both hereditary and age-related; rheumatoid arthritis, which is an auto-immune condition that primarily affects the hands, wrists and feet; spondylitis, an inflammation of the spinal vertebrae and pelvis; and gout, which occurs when there is a build-up of uric acid in the joints.

Meditation, stretching exercises and heat treatment are the first line of treatment.

REIKI TREATMENT

Treat joint areas to get energy to flow through the limbs.

Complementary treatments

- **Diet** Avoid dairy products, which build up calcium, and animal fats.
- **Exercise** Gentle stretching exercises performed daily will help to prevent stiffness.
- **Meditation** Meditate on letting go of rigid ideas and focus on the concept of being in the flow.

1 Place your hands around the joint if possible. If not, place your hands side by side over the area.

2 Use Position 15 to run energy through the legs.

BURNS AND SCALDS

The difference between burns and scalds is that burns are caused by forms of dry heat, such as fire, electricity, strong sunlight or chemicals, while scalds are caused by damp heat from boiling liquids and steam. The effects of both on the skin and soft tissues are the same, as is the treatment. You can also use this treatment for minor cuts and abrasions.

With mild burns, the damage is restricted to the outer layer of the skin and symptoms include redness, pain, heat and sometimes blistering. Mild burns are seldom very dangerous unless they cover a large area of the body. With more serious burns, the damage goes deeper into the lower layers of the skin and produces blistering. The most serious burns affect the soft tissue and the nervous system and can be difficult to treat.

Immediate treatment for a burn is to bathe the area in cold water for 10–15 minutes, and then cover it lightly with a clean cloth or bandage. Don't put anything else on the site of the burn or scald, particularly not butter or fat. Furthermore, if material is stuck to the burn, don't try to remove it yourself. You should then seek medical treatment.

Complementary treatments

- **Bach flower remedies** Rescue Remedy should be given orally to alleviate stress and shock. Usually 4 drops in water is sufficient; it can also be used to clean the wound.

- **Herbalism** Aloe vera gel may be applied to a minor burn or sunburn where the skin is unbroken. Calendula ointment will help healing after cleaning.

- **Supplements** Vitamin E oil may also be applied to minor burns after the area has been cleaned, as this prevents scarring.

REIKI TREATMENT

It is important that you don't place your hands on the wound itself, but keep them above it. In the case of a very light burn, Reiki may be sufficient treatment combined with the first-aid steps. With a burn that looks more than superficial, you should consult a doctor as soon as possible, but can give Reiki while waiting to see one. You can also use the treatment for shock (pages 98–99) immediately after the accident has happened if the person seems in need of it. Reiki can help the bleeding to stop very quickly.

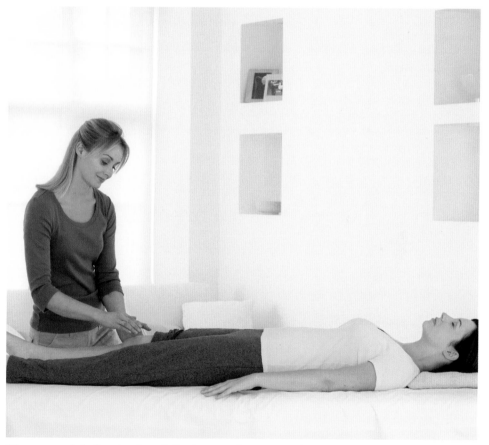

Clean wounds before treatment. For burns, minor cuts and abrasions, treat by holding your hand over the affected area.

ECZEMA

Eczema is a form of dermatitis that frequently appears in infancy or may develop in older people. In children it is often linked to hereditary causes and a disposition towards allergies. For example, children who have eczema often also have asthma and/or hay fever.

The symptoms of eczema vary in their severity according to the individual, but are characterized by patches of skin that are inflamed, itchy and scaly. In the worst cases, the skin is often broken and bleeding from being scratched. It is usually treated with soothing creams and corticosteroids, although these are to be avoided for long-term use as they cause thinning of the skin. However, in some cases they offer the only relief. People with eczema usually need to avoid highly perfumed skin and bath products, and clothes made from wool and synthetic fabrics are an irritant to the condition.

Emotionally, eczema can indicate that we are irritated by something that we desperately need to release, such as a thought pattern, in order to allow it to be replaced by something new that we feel more comfortable with.

Complementary treatments

- **Oatmeal baths** Bathing in water that has had oatmeal added to it by placing the oats inside a muslin bag is very beneficial to eczema and other dry skin conditions. There are also skin and bath products containing oats that offer relief from the symptoms.

- **Herbalism** Both Chinese and Western herbalists have a variety of plants that they use to detoxify the system and strengthen the liver and kidneys. Consult a herbalist to get the best product for you.

REIKI TREATMENT

After carrying out steps 1 and 2, you may also want to treat localized parts of the body where there is an outbreak of eczema. When doing this, don't place your hands directly on the area but hold them above it.

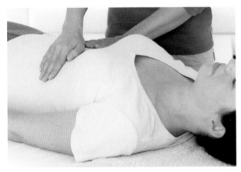

1 First treat the liver using Position 6.

2 Continue into Position 7 to further treat the liver.

3 Treat the adrenals and the kidneys using Position 14.

ACNE

Acne is an infection of the skin's sebaceous glands, which control the production of sebum, or oil, that keeps the skin from drying up. The causes of acne are most likely a combination of hormonal overproduction and diet. Foods that make the blood overly acidic are probably responsible. These include dairy products, sugar and any foods high in fats, which are typically the main components of the foods that teenagers prefer.

The teenage years are ones of emotional upheaval and the fight for independence, so it is unsurprising that acne erupts as a reflection of this struggle to be our own person. As in other conditions that involve repressed anger, the liver is a focus for treatment when using Reiki for the condition.

Complementary treatments

- **Exercise** Any exercise that releases stress, such as swimming or dancing, is beneficial. Yoga and Chi Kung will also help, as they will quieten the mind and help to improve self-image.

REIKI TREATMENT

Acne is helped by focusing on the head followed by the liver.

1 To tune into the recipient's energy flow, start by placing your hands in Position 1a.

2 Move your hands into Position 1b, taking care to keep your touch light.

3 Place your hands in Position 2a or 2b.

4 Place your hands in Position 3a. Take as much of the weight of the head as you can.

5 Slide your hands into Position 3b.

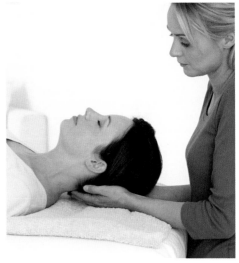

6 Hold your hands in Position 3c, again taking as much weight as you can.

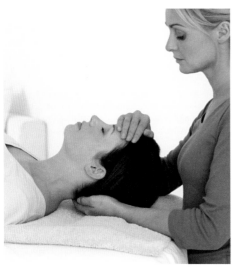

7 Place your hands in Position 4a.

8 Use Position 4b to remove your hands gently from under the recipient's head.

9   Treat the throat by placing your hands in Position 5a.

10   Pull your hands away in an arc, using Position 5b.

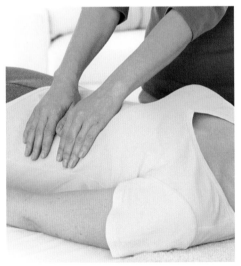

11   Place your hands in the alternative Position 6 and 7.

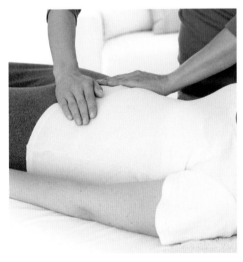

12   Place your hands in Position 8. Remember the alternative position for men.

INSECT BITES

When an insect bites you, it pierces the skin to take in blood. Our bodies respond by producing an allergic reaction at the site of the bite. Usually this just causes some redness and swelling, but some individuals may have more extreme reactions, depending on the type of insect bite. Where a reaction is more unpleasant, the person may need to take anti-histamines; otherwise cleaning the site and using a cream designed to soothe insect bites suffices.

Mosquito bites in tropical countries may lead to malaria, which will need medical treatment, but in non-tropical areas mosquito bites don't cause a problem other than itching, and are more annoying than dangerous to the victim.

Although insect bites don't constitute a condition, if they overly bother you or you find them excessively itchy, it may be that they are reflecting an underlying emotion of irritation and frustration of which you are unaware.

Nettle stings and bee or wasp stings can be treated in much the same way as insect bites as they also produce an allergic reaction. This reaction indicates that the immune system could use a boost. The Reiki treatment opposite is aimed at supporting the immune system, as well as strengthening the liver and kidneys to help the body release toxins, which leads to the itching.

In the case of a small number of people, stings send them into anaphylactic shock. This is an extremely serious allergy with a fatal result if not treated immediately with an injection of anti-histamine. Giving regular Reiki treatments to a person with this extreme allergy will help to support them, but it is important to remind them to always carry their anti-histamine.

Complementary treatments

- **Aromatherapy** Tea tree oil dabbed on the bite will help.

- **Bach flower remedies** Rescue Remedy is helpful immediately after an insect has bitten you, or you have been stung. Impatiens also helps to release feelings of irritation.

REIKI TREATMENT

The focus of this treatment is the liver and the kidneys to speed up the removal of toxins, and the thymus to strengthen the immune system.

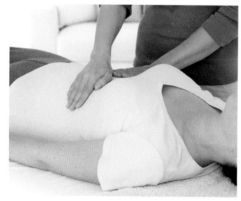

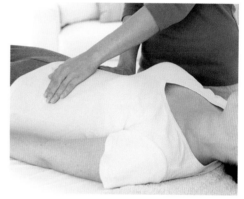

1 First, treat the liver area to release any toxins. You can use Position 6.

2 Continue into Position 7, treating the right side of the recipient's body.

3 Treat the kidneys and adrenals using Position 14.

4 Treat the thymus, which is just above the heart, to stimulate the immune system.

DANDRUFF

Dandruff is defined as the shedding of skin primarily from the scalp, and is a form of dermatitis. People with other conditions such as eczema and psoriasis, and those with dry skin in general, are probably more prone to dandruff than others. It can also be brought on by stress, and by an allergic reaction to certain shampoos. Orthodox treatment is based on anti-dandruff shampoos, although severe cases may also require the use of corticosteroids and anti-fungal treatments.

Dandruff may also be the body's way of eliminating excessive amounts of proteins and fats in the diet, which the body is unable to digest. Other suggestions are that it might be caused by too much acidic food in the diet and by imbalances in the liver and kidneys. Emotionally, dandruff may indicate an excess amount of mental energy and the desire to shed old ideas.

Complementary treatments

- **Aromatherapy** Rosemary oil is wonderful for clearing dry scalp conditions. You can massage the scalp with a base oil to which you have added a few drops of the essential oil. If you don't want to make your own, you will find ready-made oils in health-food shops or places where they sell aromatherapy products.

- **Diet** Follow a diet with low-fat animal products such as white fish, raw vegetables, which you can take in juice form, and wholegrains.

REIKI TREATMENT

The focus of the treatment is the body's elimination system: the liver and the kidneys. The adrenals are also treated to help reduce stress.

1 Place the heels of your palms on the crown of the head, fingers pointing down the side of the head.

2 Treat the adrenals and kidneys using Position 14.

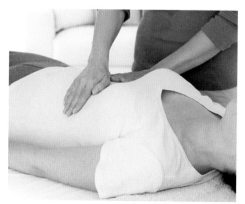

3 Place your hands over the liver area to support this organ using Position 6 or alternative Positions 6 and 7.

4 Continue treating the liver by moving into Position 7 or alternative Positions 6 and 7.

ALLERGIES

An allergic reaction occurs when the immune system responds inappropriately to an otherwise harmless substance, such as grass. This reaction can be triggered by skin contact with perhaps a chemical or animal fur, by inhaling it (as with pollen), or by eating it (as in allergies to foods ranging from eggs and nuts to strawberries).

Causes of the condition may be partially hereditary, and may be linked to other conditions such as asthma, or are the result of a weak liver and immune system, which is unable to fight the build-up of antigens (foreign substances) in the body.

Anti-histamines are used to treat some forms of allergy, such as hay fever. In severe cases, the person may need to be tested for the substances to which they are allergic, and undergo a course of desensitization treatments. With food allergies, the usual course of action is to eliminate various foods from the diet systematically, and observe the results. This usually requires consulting a nutritionist.

Emotionally, allergies are often made worse by stress of any kind. They may also be thought of as a refusal to accept personal power.

Complementary treatments

- **Diet** Consult a nutritionist to adapt your diet to identify and then manage a food allergy.

- **Exercise** Some skin conditions can improve with regular yoga.

REIKI TREATMENT

This treatment strengthens the immune system and the liver.

1 Place your hands on or over the face using Position 1.

2 Move down to treat the throat area using Position 5.

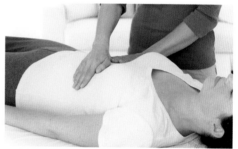

3 Place your hands horizontally below the breastbone, using Position 6.

4 Move into either Position 7, and work your way down the front of the body to treat the lungs, liver and stomach.

5 Place one hand on the thymus and the other hand on the spleen, which is in the area on the left lower ribcage.

AUTOIMMUNE DISORDERS

Immunodeficiency or auto-immune disorders are a group of conditions characterized by the fact that the immune system fails to function normally, leaving the person susceptible to infections that a normal immune system would easily fight off. The conditions may either be congenital or acquired. For example, a person born with an immunodeficiency may find that they get recurring fungal infections.

HIV is one example of acquired immunodeficiency through a viral infection; or the immune system may be suppressed due to use of certain medications. Many other conditions, such as lupus, rheumatoid arthritis, multiple sclerosis and diabetes, are also autoimmune disorders. There are no definitive medical answers as to the cause of immunodeficiency.

Emotionally, the condition could be brought on by trauma, stress and grief, all of which are known to leave even a healthy immune system somewhat weakened. As the thymus lies so close to the heart, the energy of the heart is closely associated with the condition, and it may indicate a lack of self-love and love from others.

Complementary treatments

- **Exercise** Take a yoga class, do light aerobic exercise such as walking, and find some balance in your life by setting aside time for recreational pursuits.

- **Herbalism** Consult a herbalist about herbs that will strengthen the system and help particular related conditions.

- **Supplements** Vitamins B, C and E, as well as magnesium, selenium and zinc, will strengthen the immune system.

REIKI TREATMENT

Stimulating the immune system is the first priority for a treatment followed by focusing on the areas responsible for removing infection from the body.

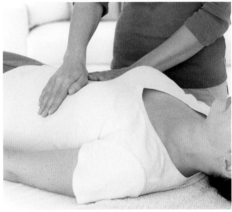

1 Place the hands over the thymus and the heart to stimulate the immune system.

2 Treat the liver, spleen and pancreas on the front of the body. Start with Position 6.

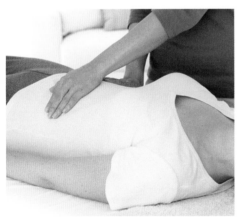

3 Move into Position 7, working down the body.

4 Treat the adrenals and kidneys with Position 14.

BACK PAIN

Back pain comes in many forms and most people experience it at some point during their life. Happily, most episodes of it can be resolved with minimum treatment; however, chronic back conditions need either ongoing treatment or intensive treatment for intermittent flare-ups.

Chronic back pain has a number of causes: damage to the coccyx, pressure on the sciatic nerve, kidney infection, degeneration of the vertebrae and discs, and pain in the back muscles. Orthodox treatment usually includes painkillers and anti-inflammatory drugs, muscle relaxants and physiotherapy.

Emotional causes vary according to the area of the back affected. For example, lower back pain is associated with feeling a lack of material support and financial concerns. The middle back is associated with feelings of guilt and being unable to receive help from others, and the upper back and neck are connected with feelings of being burdened with responsibility for others and lacking emotional support.

Complementary treatments

- **Aromatherapy** Using oils such as camomile and eucalyptus put on hot compresses followed by cold compresses and held over the inflamed area will reduce back pain and swelling.

- **Massage and hydrotherapy** These are excellent ways to reduce inflammation.

- **Pilates** Consult a qualified Pilates instructor about specific exercises for your condition. Pilates has been very successful in helping many people with chronic back pain.

REIKI TREATMENT

Treat the entire back, focusing on the area of most pain. This may mean adding some hand positions to cover the coccyx at the base of the spine, and also the sciatic nerve.

1 To treat the coccyx, place both hands over the tailbone. You can place your hands on top of one another, or place them side by side

2 To treat the sciatic nerve, place both hands on the outer part of the right buttock. Repeat this on the outer part of the left buttock.

3 Use Position 15 on both legs to run the energy from the soles of the feet to the spine and back.

SINUSITIS

The sinuses are pockets of air space around the nasal cavity. Sinusitis is a fairly common condition that is mostly an acute one, but in some people it becomes a chronic condition. Orthodox methods of treating it are with nasal decongestants, antibiotics and occasionally, if the condition is severe, by draining the sinuses surgically.

Symptoms of sinusitis are pain around the nasal area and in the centre of the forehead along with the feeling of being unable to breathe properly.

Emotionally, we may be holding on to a deep mental conflict that we are unable to communicate to anyone, which results in us blocking it up and only releasing it drop by drop.

Complementary treatments

- **Acupressure and acupuncture** These may help to clear blockages in the lymph system.

- **Diet** Remove all dairy products from your diet for a week. This will help to clear mucus from the system.

- **Aromatherapy** Inhaling oils such as eucalyptus in hot water will help to clear the nasal passages. You could also consider having aromatherapy massages to treat the emotional causes.

REIKI TREATMENT

Focus on the sinuses to relieve congestion and on the liver to remove toxins.

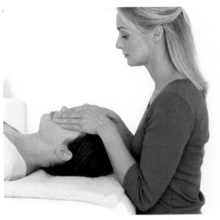

1 Place your hands over the face, using Position 1b.

2 Place one hand across the forehead. See Position 4a.

3 Treat the liver and spleen on the front of the body to help release toxic build-up. First use Position 6.

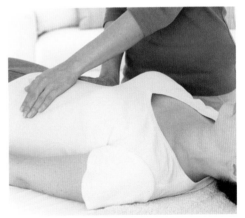

4 Continue into Position 7 or alternative Position 7, working down the body.

MENSTRUAL PROBLEMS

Menstruation relies on a combination of the development of the uterus lining and the regulation of hormone production. Problems arise when this delicate mechanism is not in balance. Problems manifest in different ways, the most common of which is dysmenorrhoea, usually called painful periods.

The absence of menstruation, although normal during pregnancy, at other times is caused by anorexia and stress. Menorrhagia, which is characterized by excessive bleeding, is usually caused by a hormone imbalance and the presence of fibroids or polyps in the uterus.

Emotionally, menstrual problems point to a conflict with a woman's female nature.

REIKI TREATMENT

Treatments focus on the pelvic area and lower chakras.

Complementary treatments

- **Aromatherapy** Add a few drops of clary sage to the bath. Or consult an aromatherapist as some oils produce dramatic effects.

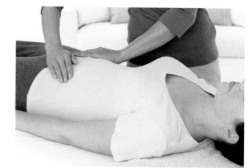

1 Treat the pelvic area, using Position 8. If self-treating, you may wish to treat the pubic area.

2 Treat the lower back by placing the hands in the centre of the back over the tailbone.

PROSTATE PROBLEMS

The prostate gland is located at the opening of the urethra in men and is responsible for secreting the fluid that carries semen at the point of ejaculation. The prostate can become inflamed through bacterial infection, which is usually a sexually transmitted infection. This is treated with antibiotics. In older men, there is a tendency for the prostate to become enlarged. This causes blockages in the urethra and difficulties with urination. Surgery may be needed to rectify the problem.

Stress is a cause of the prostate problems, as is a diet that is high in animal protein and saturated fats.

Emotionally, prostate problems may signal a feeling of impotence and frustration with sexual performance.

Complementary treatments

- **Meditation** This will help you to relieve stress and to accept the ageing process.

- **Yoga** A regular routine will relax the mind, and certain exercises strengthen the pelvic area.

REIKI TREATMENT

Treat men for this as a matter of routine to prevent the condition.

1 With the recipient on his front, place one hand horizontally across the tailbone, and the other at a right angle to it, with the fingers pointing down the centre of the buttocks. You can also place one hand on top of the other to cover this same area.

INFERTILITY

Infertility may result from problems in either the male or female reproductive systems. Male infertility may be caused by blockages in the reproductive system, sexually transmitted diseases, genetic disorders, or low sperm count caused by stress, smoking and some drugs. Female infertility is caused by blocked fallopian tubes, the ovaries not releasing eggs, problems with the uterus that prevent implantation, and cervical mucus that destroys sperm.

Emotionally, couples with infertility problems may have issues with being in the present moment, and dwell too much on the past or future.

REIKI TREATMENT

Treatment focuses on the reproductive organs.

1 To treat the reproductive organs, use Position 8 for women. For men, treat the groin area.

Complementary treatments

- **Diet** It is best to consult a nutritionist about following a diet that balances the body energy.

- **Exercise** Any exercise that decreases stress and promotes mental and physical balance is beneficial. Swimming, walking, yoga and Chi Kung are ideal.

2 Treat the adrenal glands and kidneys using Position 14.

EAR INFECTIONS

Ear infections tend to be more prevalent among children, but adults may also experience them. Otitis media, an infection of the middle ear, is very common in children. Other types of ear infection are: otitis externa, which happens in the ear canal; mastoiditis, in which pain is experienced in the bone behind the ear; and labyrinthitis, which is an infection of the inner ear. Earache can also be caused by referred pain from the teeth and jaw.

Emotionally, an ear infection may indicate that we don't like what we are hearing and want to block it out.

REIKI TREATMENT

Treatment concentrates on the ears and their connection with the throat.

1 Place your hands over the ears with your palms covering the opening using Position 2a.

Complementary treatments

- **Diet** Remove dairy and wheat products, meat and sugar from the diet, and any other foods known to be mucus-forming. Replace these foods with fruit and vegetable juices and plain foods such as steamed rice.

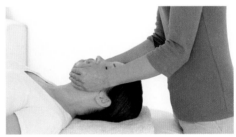

2 Then place your hands along the jawline, which will treat the connection between the ears and the throat.

ASTHMA

The number of people suffering from this condition, which is potentially life-threatening, continues to increase in many countries. It is caused by an inflammation of bronchi and bronchioles, resulting in constriction in the lungs, plus an increase in production of mucus, which narrows the airways. Symptoms include breathlessness, wheezing and coughing.

An attack can be triggered by allergens such as dust and pollen, by exercise and even by strong winds. Stress is another trigger, and girls and women may notice that their asthma gets worse for a few days before menstruation, indicating a hormonal link. Asthma usually develops in childhood and is often hereditary, but frequently clears up, or at least decreases in severity, once the adult years begin. However, it can suddenly develop in adults who have no previous experience of it.

Nutritionally, it is thought to be linked to an excess of dairy products and wheat in the diet. There is also a suggestion that it is more prevalent in children who are not breastfed or who are weaned too early.

Emotionally, it is connected to 'overmothering', which leads to the child literally feeling smothered and unable to find space to be themself.

Complementary treatments

- **Diet** Remove dairy and wheat products from the diet, and limit the amount of carbonated drinks children have, as these promote the production of mucus. Some food colourings may also exacerbate asthma.

- **Exercise** Learning the breathing techniques of either Chi Kung or yoga can help enormously with alleviating an attack or preventing the onset of asthma.

REIKI TREATMENT

When treating someone during an attack it is preferable to prop them up with pillows on a sofa, or sit them on an upright chair.

1 Sitting behind the person, lay your hands below the throat in a V-shape with palms on the collarbone.

2 Place one hand on the thymus and another on the spleen, on the left side of the body.

3 Place the hands horizontally across the upper chest. Keeping your hands in the same position, work down the entire chest area.

4 Move into Position 14. In Chinese medicine, weak kidney function is thought to cause asthma.

THE COMMON COLD

There are very few people who have not had a cold at some time or other. Some people are particularly susceptible to colds and become infected several times a year. A cold is basically an infection of the linings of the nose and throat, and its familiar symptoms are nasal congestion, headache, sore throat, a runny nose and a cough.

Colds are caused by viruses and treatment is according to the symptoms, which is why many households have an array of painkillers, nasal decongestants, cough medicines and throat lozenges in their cupboards. These, combined with rest and fluids to flush out the infection, are usually sufficient treatment.

Emotionally, a cold may be a sign that you need to slow down and take a rest.

REIKI TREATMENT

Treatment focuses on the immune system, areas of infection and clearing toxins.

Complementary treatments

- **Supplements** Increase your intake of Vitamin C and zinc while you have a cold, and ensure that these are part of your regular diet to prevent colds. Echinacea is also beneficial for both treatment and prevention.

1 Place the hands over the face as in Position 1.

2 Then place your hands over or around the throat area using Position 5.

3 Place your hands horizontally across the upper chest. In self-treatments hands may be placed on the breasts.

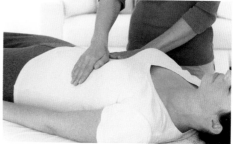

4 Treat the liver and spleen. Start with Position 6.

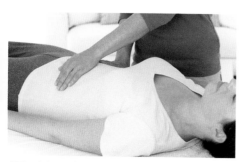

5 Move into Position 7 and work down the body.

6 Place your hands over the thymus to strengthen the immune system.

EYE PROBLEMS

There are many forms of eye problems, ranging from blindness at one extreme to simple eye strain at the other. In between there are astigmatism, strabismus (squint), short-sightedness and long-sightedness. These are all related to the refraction of light as it passes through the lens of the eye.

For example, a short-sighted person can see objects close to them quite clearly, while anything in the distance is a blur. A long-sighted person experiences this in reverse. An astigmatism is the result of a malformed cornea, causing blurred images. A squint is caused by under- or overdeveloped eye muscles that alter normal vision. Eye strain is frequently experienced by those using computers for long periods of time without rest, and by those in professions that require focused reading of text and numerals.

The usual treatment for eye problems is to use glasses or contact lenses to correct vision. Laser treatment is also possible for more severe eyesight problems. Orthodox medicine does not recognize common eye problems that are unrelated to other conditions as having any root cause other than natural decline as part of the ageing process, or overuse of the eyes as part of work. Chinese medicine, on the other hand, indicates that a weakened liver function is responsible for decline in eyesight.

Emotionally, each type of eye problem has a different cause, but in general it is a refusal to see something. For example, a short-sighted person may only want to see what is in front of them, while a long-sighted person prefers not to see what is personal or close to them and spends their time looking into the future.

Complementary treatments

- **Acupuncture** This will stimulate the liver.

- **Exercise** There are several Chi Kung exercises specifically designed to strengthen the eyes, as well as exercises for the liver.

REIKI TREATMENT

Concentrate treatment on the eyes and head, and on the liver to clear toxins.

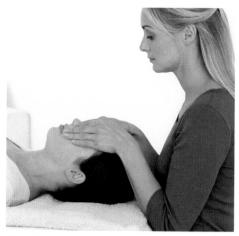

1 Place your hands over the eyes using Position 1b.

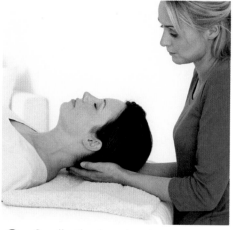

2 Cradle the head, using Position 3c.

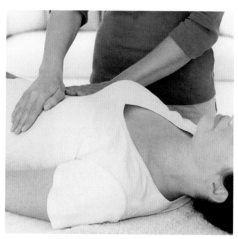

3 Treat the liver by using Position 6.

4 Use Position 7 to complete treatment of the liver.

ANXIETY

Most people experience a certain amount of anxiety, but when it becomes a dominant response to living it is unhealthy. Anxiety is a broad term that covers a range of emotions from mild unease to intense fear. The root causes of anxiety vary from learned responses to specific situations to unconscious internal conflicts, or a physiological response to events as a result of overstimulation of the central nervous system.

The condition produces a broad spectrum of symptoms ranging from the mild to the severe. Many people having an anxiety attack may experience palpitations, chest pain and constricted breathing, and feel as if they are having a heart attack. Other general symptoms are nausea, sleeplessness, diarrhoea and loss of appetite combined with irritability, irrational fears and extreme pessimism. Orthodox methods of treating the condition are psychotherapy or counselling and, for some symptoms, medication.

Emotionally, anxiety represents a sense of being alone in the world. A person with anxiety does not trust the process of living and has lost faith that the Universe always provides solutions to all situations.

Complementary treatments

- **Bach flower remedies** Use Rescue Remedy when you feel anxiety building up or when having a panic attack.

- **Exercise** Practise yoga or Chi Kung regularly to reduce stress and anxiety.

- **Meditation** Regular meditation on connection to the Universe or to God or whatever you consider to be the creative energy of the Universe, will reduce any feelings of separation.

REIKI TREATMENT

This sequence balances the adrenals, which increase adrenalin production when we are anxious and become quickly exhausted.

1 Place the heels of your palms on the crown of the head, fingertips pointing down in front of the ears.

2 Treat the front of the body, starting with Position 6 at the solar plexus.

3 Work down to cover the liver, spleen, pancreas and stomach using Position 7.

4 On the back, treat the adrenals and kidneys using Position 14.

FATIGUE

Fatigue is a common condition in the modern world that is characterized by more than simply feeling tired. It is a collection of symptoms that includes tiredness along with lethargy and lack of motivation. Fatigue is caused by sleeplessness, and therefore may accompany insomnia, but it is caused by a poor diet as well. It may also be caused by underlying disorders such as anaemia, depression, anxiety and cancer; therefore persistent fatigue should be investigated by a doctor.

It may be treated by a change in diet, adding more foods that are rich in iron, folic acid and Vitamin B12. These can also be taken as supplements. Rest is also important. Fatigue is a sign that we have done too much and as a result are out of balance. We have probably given too much time to activities that require us to expend energy, such as work, and have not taken the time to restore ourselves with activities that nourish us in body, mind and spirit, such as meditation, painting, reading and taking care of our bodies in a loving way. As a result, our minds and bodies never get to relax fully, and we become depleted of energy. Fatigue is a message from mind, body and spirit to change your lifestyle and find balance in your life.

Complementary treatments

- **Aromatherapy** Have regular aromatherapy massages to stimulate the body, but also to relax it.

- **Exercise** Gentle exercise such as walking, yoga and Chi Kung will help release mental and physical stress.

- **Meditation** Use meditation to release mental stress.

REIKI TREATMENT

As with all conditions, it is best to give a full treatment if possible, but you can focus on areas that are particularly affected by stress to help fatigue.

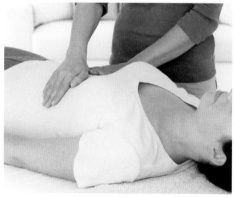

1 Place one hand over the thymus and the other hand over the spleen on the left hand side of the body.

2 Place the hands across the front of the body, covering the solar plexus using Position 6.

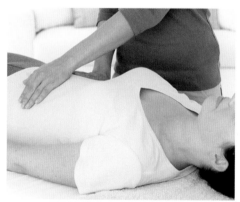

3 Move your hands one hand-width down to Position 7.

4 Treat the adrenals and kidneys on the back using Position 14.

HEADACHES

Headaches are caused by constriction of the blood vessels in the lining of the brain and by tension in the scalp. Different types of pain may be experienced, varying from a dull, throbbing ache to the deep, sharp type.

The main cause of headaches is usually stress or tension caused by emotional factors; or they may be caused by environmental factors, such as poor lighting or diet. Most headaches pass quickly, and can be treated with painkillers, but persistent headaches may point to an underlying condition and you should seek medical treatment for them.

Emotionally, a headache is a symptom of an overloaded mind.

Complementary treatments

- **Aromatherapy** Rubbing lavender oil onto the temples reduces pain and promotes relaxation.

- **Massage** An Indian head massage or a full body massage will help to work on the root causes of the headache.

REIKI TREATMENT

Treat the head and follow with stress-affected areas such as the solar plexus.

1 Treat the head. Start by using Position 1b.

2 Continue treating the head, using Position 2a.

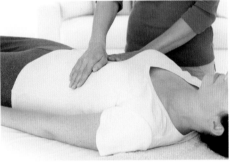

3 Treat the spleen, liver and stomach. Start with Position 6.

4 Contune treating the area by moving into Position 7.

5 Treat the adrenals and kidneys on the back using Position 14.

INSOMNIA

Insomniacs find it difficult to fall asleep or to stay asleep. Most people experience insomnia briefly at some point in their lives, usually in response to a stressful situation. However, for some people it turns into a chronic condition that may last for years. The causes of insomnia are frequently underlying conditions such as depression and anxiety, and drug users are also likely to experience it during withdrawal. It may be related to lifestyle factors such as shift work, excessive caffeine intake and lack of exercise.

Insomnia is usually treated by establishing a more regulated lifestyle including a regular time for going to bed, but insomnia caused by depression may be more difficult to treat and require a number of approaches, including medication and counselling or psychotherapy. Chinese medicine and other healing methods see insomnia as indicating a weakness in the liver and gallbladder, and treatment focuses on these organs.

Emotionally, a person with insomnia may be feeling unable to surrender or be vulnerable, which is what we are when we are sleeping. They are also unable to trust life and fear for their survival.

Complementary treatments

- **Aromatherapy** As well as having aromatherapy massages, you can use a variety of oils at home either in the bath or to scent the bedroom. Consult an aromatherapist about the oils that will work best for you. Lavender is the standard oil for relaxation, and you could also try patchouli and benzoin, both of which are grounding.

- **Exercise** Some form of daily exercise such as walking will help with relaxation.

- **Herbalism** Drink herbal teas such as camomile and rosehip to calm and soothe the nerves.

REIKI TREATMENT

These positions are also ideal for self-treatment of insomnia. For maximum benefit, give treatments just before bedtime, if possible.

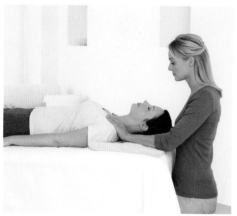

1 Start by placing your hands in Position 1a to tune into the recipient's energy flow.

2 Move into Position 1b by lowering your hands onto the recipient's face.

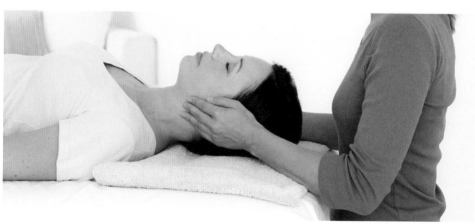

3 Place your hands in Position 2a.

4 Gently move into Position 3a, rolling the head to the right.

5 Move your hands into Position 3b.

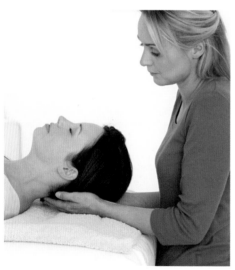

6 Slowly roll the head back to the centre, using Position 3c.

7 Keeping your left hand in place, move your right hand to lie across the forehead in Position 4a.

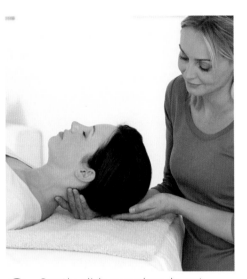

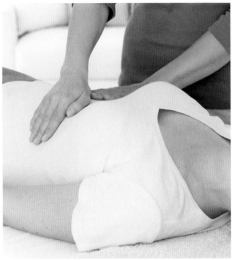

8 Gently slide your hands out from under the head, as in Position 4b.

9 Place your hands one behind the other beneath the chest area, as in Position 6.

10 To finish, slide your hands into Position 7. It is likely that the person will be deeply relaxed, a state that is restorative.

REIKI AND
OTHER THERAPIES

A number of complementary therapies can be used alongside Reiki. The most popular feature on the following pages.

ACUPUNCTURE

Acupuncture is one of the oldest healing methods in the world and is one of the best-known components of Traditional Chinese Medicine (TCM). It works by stimulating specific points on the meridians (see pages 36–39) using very fine, metal needles to pierce the skin. This is not as painful as it sounds. The needles are then manipulated manually by the acupuncturist.

The aim of acupuncture is to bring the elements of Yin and Yang into a state of balance. Yin is characterized by cold, passive energy and femaleness, while Yang is hot, active energy associated with maleness. When Yin and Yang are not balanced, blockages in the flow of Ki around the meridians occur, and these then manifest as disease. The insertion of the needles removes the blockages.

Acupuncture is now widely used by orthodox medical practitioners as well as those working in complementary practices, and also by many physiotherapists.

Acupuncture is used to treat a wide range of conditions, and has proved to be particularly effective for back pain and pain control in general. It is sometimes used to relieve nausea following chemotherapy and has also helped some people to free themselves from addictions such as smoking and drugs.

ACUPUNCTURE AND REIKI

Alternating Reiki treatments with acupuncture will not reduce the effectiveness of either. Indeed, the Reiki will enhance the acupuncture by supporting the removal of blockages in the meridians.

CAUTION

There are some basic guidelines you should observe:

First, ensure that the acupuncturist is properly trained and has certificates to prove it. Often personal recommendation is the best way to find an acupuncturist.

You should also make sure that the acupuncturist uses disposable needles from sealed packets.

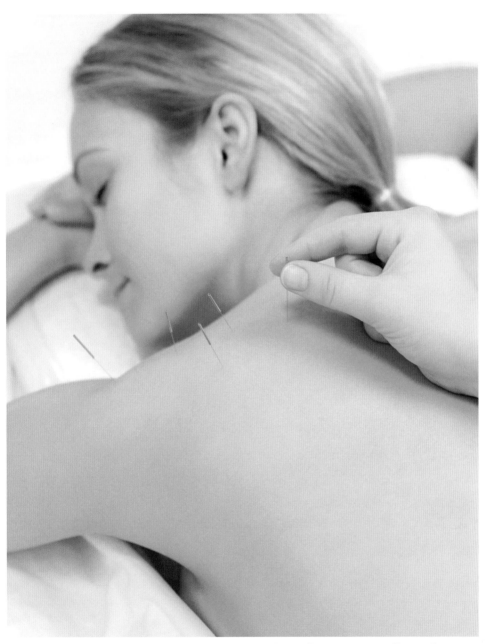

Acupuncture helps to remove blockages in the meridians, allowing the Ki to flow with ease once more.

AROMATHERAPY

Aromatherapy is an ancient art, but the modern practice of using distilled oils for healing was developed in the 1920s by French chemist René-Maurice Gattefossé. He had a perfume laboratory and one day, having burned himself, he plunged his arm into the nearest available cold liquid, which happened to be lavender oil. He then observed that the pain decreased, the burn healed more quickly than usual and there was little or no scarring. This prompted him to investigate the healing properties of other plant and fruit oils.

Essential oils stimulate parts of the brain linked to emotions, each working to support positive changes in your body.

Aromatherapy involves the treatment or prevention of disease with essential oils. These can be used in a number of ways. You can add them to your bath or add them to a base oil and massage in; both these methods work on absorption of the oils through the skin. The other method of use is inhaling them, either by using an oil burner or by adding them to hot water and inhaling the steam. Using them in the bath or inhaling them are the most popular methods of home use of oils, while aromatherapists tend to combine their use with massage.

Orthodox medicine does not give much credence to aromatherapy other than to accept that it promotes relaxation. This attitude is based on the fact that it has proved very difficult to conduct studies on it that are acceptably scientific for the medical community. Physiologically, there are two possible explanations for how it works and why it does heal both physical and emotional conditions. The first theory is that the aromas stimulate the limbic system in the brain. This is linked to the olfactory system and supports the emotions. The other explanation is that the plant essences have a pharmacological effect, just as they do in herbalism.

Aromatherapy is safe, although caution must be taken during pregnancy.

Useful oils to have at home

If you are buying oils to use at home, beware of cheap brands as they will not bring any benefits and are only useful as room scenters. You should always look for oils that are of a therapeutic grade. The oils vary in price – those made from commonly available plants, such as lavender or pine, are significantly cheaper than rarer ones, such as pure rose oil.

- **Anti-bacterial oils** – rosemary, tea tree
- **Anti-depressive oils** – lavender, rose
- **Anti-fungal oils** – lavender, juniper
- **Anti-inflammatory oils** – eucalyptus
- **Anti-viral oils** – lemongrass, sandalwood, thyme

AROMATHERAPY AND REIKI

Aromatherapists frequently combine Reiki hand treatments with a massage, because the two complement each other. Used together in this way, they intensify the effects of both practices.

MASSAGE

Massage is the manipulation of the soft body tissues. Massage can be used on every body part from head to foot, and it focuses on muscles, tendons, connective tissues and the lymphatic system.

Massage has been adopted by orthodox medicine for a wide range of physical conditions involving the muscles and joints, and it is also valued for its effects on stress, depression and anxiety.

TYPES OF MASSAGE

A bewildering array of massage types is available now. Some of the most commonly found are described here.

Swedish massage
One of the best known and widely available types, this is based on five types of strokes. It is effective in treating stiffness in the joints.

Shiatsu
A Japanese method of massage that uses thumb pressure to work along the meridians, in a similar way to acupressure. Part of the method also includes stretching the limbs. This method is very suited to treating the emotional root cause of a range of physical conditions.

Massage is well established as an effective form of treatment for a wide range of physical conditions.

Indian head massage is very popular and helps to balance the chakras.

Thai massage

Thai massage treatments are generally longer than the average massage treatment. They are based on yoga, and during the treatment the body will be manipulated into yoga-like postures. As in shiatsu, thumb pressure is also applied to specific points. It is very useful for releasing energy blocks and restoring balance.

Bowen therapy

Developed by Tom Bowen, this technique involves a rolling movement over the muscles, tendons and joints. It is beneficial for releasing muscle tension and improving lymphatic flow.

Indian head massage ('champissage')

This type focuses on the head, face and shoulders, and releases tension in all the muscles in that area. Its primary use is to balance the chakras.

MASSAGE AND REIKI

In a similar way to that of aromatherapy practices (see pages 160–161), Reiki hand treatments combine very effectively with all kinds of massage. The hands can channel the energy while also physically delivering the massage to the recipient.

BACH FLOWERS

This range of remedies was developed by Dr Edward Bach, a medical practitioner. His interest in homeopathy and his natural gift as a healer led him to seek purer alternatives to the traditional homeopathic medicines that are based on treating disease with the products of that disease, often described as 'treating like with like'. Bach remedies are very useful for treatment of children as well as adults, and there are no known adverse effects.

The philosophy behind his system is one of treating the mental and emotional states of the patient in order to heal physical symptoms. Using his intuition, he created a set of 38 plant remedies for treating emotional states. The remedies are made by two methods: floating the blooms in pure water for several hours, or boiling them for half an hour. They are then combined with pure brandy to preserve them on a 50/50 ratio. A practitioner will be able to advise you on the remedy, or combination of remedies, for your specific emotional state.

TAKING THE REMEDIES

You can either drop the remedies straight onto the tongue, or dilute 4 drops in 30 ml water and drink it, four times a day.

Useful remedies at home

- **Elm** – when feeling overwhelmed by responsibility

- **Gorse** – when experiencing a sense of hopelessness or despair

- **Olive** – for exhaustion following mental or physical effort

- **Rescue Remedy** – the most famous of the Bach products, this was developed by Dr Bach as an emotional first-aid kit based on his observation of the typical emotional reactions to crisis

- **Star of Bethlehem** – used to treat shock

Flower remedies have no known adverse effects, making them ideal for children.

YOGA

One of the advantages of yoga is that, as with Reiki, it is a practice you can do yourself. Added to this, the yoga postures not only work on the energy body, but also stretch the physical body, ensuring that mobility can be maintained for longer as you age.

Yoga originates from ancient Indian texts that describe the philosophy behind the practice and the postures (*Asanas*), breathing practices and forms of meditation.

Although yoga may seem strenuous for those with musculoskeletal problems, an experienced teacher can adapt the postures to include them in classes, or run ones specifically for people who need a much gentler form of yoga. .

Yoga works to balance the chakras as the postures aim to free up the movement of *Ki* around the body. This is called *Prana* in the yoga tradition. Through a set of postures that work the entire body, the *Kundalini* energy stored at the base of the spine rises up through each chakra until it reaches the crown chakra. Being able to bring the energy up to the crown leads to *Samadhi*, and this is when we are able to experience unity with the universal spirit.

Hatha yoga

Hatha yoga is based on adopting physical postures. There are several forms, the three best-known ones being Iyengar, Ashtanga and Sivananda. A popular new form is Bikram, which is very physical and performed in rooms kept at high temperatures to encourage sweating.

Iyengar This form of yoga focuses on achieving the correct body alignment for each posture, and uses a variety of props such as straps and blankets to enable the student to achieve advanced poses.

Ashtanga A very active form of yoga that is challenging for the beginner, this form focuses on the strength and flexibility of the student and on all the movements being synchronized with the breath.

Sivananda This focuses on working the solar plexus area. It combines the use of postures with breathing techniques, diet and meditation.

Yoga balances the chakras and improves the flow of Ki around the body.

CHI KUNG

Like acupuncture, Chi Kung is one of the pillars of Traditional Chinese Medicine (TCM). The name means 'energy cultivation'. It is similar to yoga in that it uses body movement and breathing to improve the flow of energy around the body, but it is less extreme in its body postures and therefore may be more suitable for those of limited mobility, or people who enjoy slower, more meditative movements.

The origins, theory and practice of Chi Kung can be found in *The Yellow Emperor's Classic of Internal Medicine*, a medical text written around the 3rd century BCE. It only appeared even more recently in the West, but is now growing in popularity, along with Tai Chi, which is a related practice but uses a longer series of steps in its exercises.

By using gentle stretching exercises combined with breathing techniques and visualization, Chi Kung balances the Chi. Its primary aim is to prevent disease and promote longevity.

THE TAOIST TRADITION

There are many styles of Chi Kung, stemming from five main traditions: Taoist, Buddhist, Confucian, martial arts and medical. Of these, it is the Taoist philosophy that forms the roots of Chi Kung. This philosophy has an organic view of the world, which centres around the need to be in harmony with the Tao. The Tao is something that is transcendent and cannot be explained – it just is. Chi Kung is a path to that state of harmony that is ´being in the Tao´.

CHI KUNG AND REIKI

Reiki practitioners will find Chi Kung easy to practise because of prior knowledge of working with energy. Practising Chi Kung improves your understanding of the way Reiki works from a different perspective, and therefore enhances your ability to work with it. You can also do distance healing with Chi Kung once you have been practising it for some time. I used to exchange distance healing with my Chi Kung teacher – I used Reiki and she used Chi Kung. I could feel the energy just as intensely as if she had been sending Reiki.

Chi Kung improves the flow of energy around the body and is particularly suitable for people with limited mobility.

CRYSTAL THERAPY

Throughout history, crystals and gems have been used for therapeutic purposes. They are once again extremely popular, and many people buy them not just for their healing powers but also for their beauty. As with plants, food and colours, each gem or crystal has an energy vibration unique to its type, and this can be utilized to balance energy.

Crystals need to be cleansed before use, and at regular intervals, and you should consult various sources for information on this and on the properties of all the various types of crystals. Whether you buy your crystals in their original rough state, or after having been cut and polished, does not affect their power, so it is entirely a matter of personal preference.

Crystals can be used in various ways. Chakra therapists often place them on the body, using a different crystal for each chakra. In The Chakra Bible, Patricia Mercier gives detailed information on the appropriate crystals to use for each chakra that will activate, calm or balance them.

POPULAR CRYSTALS

The most popular types of crystals are ones from the quartz family. The structure of these stones makes them more effective at holding healing energies. Amethyst and rose quartz are widely available.

Amethyst

This is thought to be a powerful aid to spiritual advancement that promotes feelings of divine love, intuition and creative inspiration, as it works with the pineal and pituitary glands and right-brain activities. Physically, it supports the endocrine and immune systems.

Rose quartz

Often referred to as the 'love stone', this promotes forgiveness and compassion and restores emotional balance by helping us release anger and fear. Physically, it works with the spleen, kidneys, heart, circulation and reproductive system.

The popularity of crystals is both based on their beauty and on their ability to alleviate various conditions.

CRYSTALS AND REIKI

Although the use of crystals is not part of the original Reiki system, many teachers and practitioners now use them as an addition to treatments. Reiki practitioners using crystals often make crystal grids, which they then place in the room they use for giving treatments. The crystals are charged with Reiki and are thought to amplify the Reiki energy. Details about how to make these can be found in Penelope Quest's book *Reiki for Life*.

INDEX

PICTURE CREDITS

Commissioned Photography
© Octopus Publishing Group Limited/Ruth Jenkinson

Other Photography:
AKG F. Kunst & Geschichte 17;
Alamy Geoffrey Kidd 165; Matthew Mawson 56;
Corbis UK Ltd Luca Tettoni 171;
Getty Images Image Source 18, 160; Marcy Maloy 49;
Octopus Publishing Group Limited/Frazer Cunningham 34;
Ruth Jenkinson 41, 21, 62, 91, 92, 167, 169; William Reavell 28;
Photolibrary Matthew Wakem 7;
Royalty-Free Images 13;
Shutterstock velora 9; Yanik Chauvin 159, 162, 163.